At Work With Human Puzzles

Image copyrights
Front Cover Image: 2008 © LuMaxArt – Scott Maxwell. Image from BigStockPhoto.com
Back Cover Image and TOC: 2008 © LuMaxArt – Scott Maxwell. Image from BigStockPhoto.com
Page 104: Remote Image. 2007 © Ivan Josifovic. Image from BigStockPhoto.com
Page 4 & 7: Workforce Image. 2006 © Michael Darcy Brown. Image from BigStockPhoto.com
Page 4 & 37: Business Woman Image. 2009 © Carlos Seller. Image from BigStockPhoto.com
Page 104: Light bulb Image. 2005 © Tom Schmucker. Image from BigStockPhoto.com
Page 4 & 95: Project schedule Image. 2008 © Marzky Ragma Jr.. Image from BigStockPhoto.com
Page 4 & 57: Interface Image. 2009 © Daniel Kaesler. Image from BigStockPhoto.com

Library of Congress Control Number (LCCN): 2010903356

Printed by CreateSpace: Charleston, South Carolina, United States

At Work With Human Puzzles

What's So Puzzling About People at Work? 1

Puzzle Piece 1: Personnel 7

    Why is Knowledge of People Important to Personnel
    Processes?...8
    Personnel Selection 9
        Motivation..10
        What Personnel Selection Means to You, a
        Business Manager...11
        Round Pegs and Round Holes – Matching People
        and Jobs 13
        So, What About Interviews?..15
    Defining Human Abilities and Characteristics....................17
    Examples of Taxonomies 19
        Abilities..20
        Personality 25
        Behavior..28
        Interests..29
    Putting This Knowledge to Use 30
        Measuring Human Characteristics......................................32
    Personnel Recap 35

Puzzle Piece 2: Training and Expertise 37

    Why is Knowledge of People Important to Training? 38
    Expertise Progression...38
        Competency 39
        Mastery 39
        Stages of Education 43
    Training Implementation...47
        Competence Building 48
        Expertise Building 50

Organizational Knowledge Sharing 53
Training and Expertise Recap 55

Puzzle Piece 3: Technology Insertion and Interface Design 57

Why is Knowledge of People Important to Technology
Insertion and Interface Design? 58
Humans as Part of a System 58
Human Behavior 61
Adaptation 66
    Adaptation Theory 66
    Adaptation in Business 71
Designing the Machine Interface 73
    A Word on Guidelines 76
    Metrics 79
Automation 81
    A Comparison of Systems 85
    The Need for System "Integration" 88
    Focusing on the User Experience 89
Technology Insertion and Interface Design Recap 93

Puzzle Piece 4: Systems Engineering 95

Why is Knowledge of People Important to Systems
Engineering? 96
Integrating HSI Techniques into the Systems
Engineering Process 99
A Detailed Look at Techniques 105
    User Descriptions 106
    Use Cases and Exceptions – the Key to Designing
    for Flexibility 107
    Usability Testing 109
System Engineering Coordination - Legitimizing HSI
Through Risks and Requirements 114
Systems Engineering: Customer Relations 118
Why Human Systems Integration is Easy 119
Why Human Systems Integration is Hard 119

Systems Engineering Recap 121

References 123

Index 127

About the Author 129

Parting Notes 129

What's So Puzzling About People at Work?

When asked what you do for a living, you most likely reply with a brief title, and if there is interest describe the technical or process aspects of your job. These are the things you studied in school and are the basis of what you were hired to do. The "other" aspect of your job, dealing with people, was less studied, spelled out, and often, well, puzzling. In fact, often the most difficult business problems to solve revolve around people rather than technologies and processes. We wonder why organizations and co-workers act the way they do. We get frustrated trying to use a new product. We can't quite put our finger on how to design our website so that people will return. We know the common thread to these problems is people, but what is it about them that we need to know? How do we dissect our view of people in order to come to a conclusion on what action to take? Often these issues seem ill-defined and vague. Or sometimes we understand them at a high level, only to find that the situation gets more complex when delving into details. We all have a general notion of what makes a good webpage, what constitutes good training, and how to conduct good employment interviews. But questions arise when it comes down to defining what is good versus not good at a detailed level. How do we know that our website is usable? How do we know our training is effective? How can we be confident that we've selected the right person for the job?

Finding the answers to these questions is similar to other problem solving situations where there is incomplete information. In work settings, you may notice people using pictures of clouds in PowerPoint presentations to represent networks or processes where information is either unknown or too large to be detailed in the presentation. This simplifies the presentation and alleviates the need to address the intricacies behind the concept. Ironically, the cloud can also be an accurate metaphor of how much is truly understood about the subject. Ideas about how to define and approach the subject may be truly nebulous. This cloud continues to obscure until someone with enough expertise can provide a meaningful way to structure the problem set and approach. This book is about clearing clouds away from business problems involving the human element. The goal is to use human characteristics as the pieces of the puzzle which will be used to solve your personnel, training, interface design, and systems puzzles.

The most widely used way to summarize human characteristics in the context of the workplace is through knowledge, skills, abilities, and other personal characteristics, conveniently referred to as KSAOs. These provide a common denominator to anchor the ensuing discussion. The following descriptions provide sufficient distinction for the depth of this discussion:

- Knowledge is the set of information needed to perform the target task, duty, or job.
- Skills are similar to knowledge in that they are acquired through training, practice, or maturation. They may be combined with knowledge and mediated by abilities to result in performance of a given task or job. They typically go beyond knowledge to help the individual perform in an expressive manner, whether it is physical performance or producing some kind of intellectual product.
- Abilities are an individual's inherent characteristics that define performance potential. Inherency is the key distinction between abilities and skill.[1]
- Other personal characteristics are the remaining personality and attitude characteristics that influence learning and performance motivation. Although somewhat harder to define, much light has been shed on this area in the past few decades.

---

[1] As with most subjects in the field of psychology, there is debate about whether abilities are truly innate or whether they can be acquired with experience. For the sake of simplicity, I have avoided this argument and treated abilities as being primarily innate.

While all these are needed to create a complete picture, this book focuses mainly on abilities and human behavior. While knowledge and skills must be defined in employment and training environments, we are more interested in uncovering the persistent human ability, personality, and behavioral traits. By knowing these we can better understand how people will perform in the workplace, learn, and behave when using new technologies.

This book is written for business professionals and students in the field of human factors, industrial/organizational psychology, and other areas of applied psychology. For professionals, I address some key people-related problems business people face and provide frameworks for understanding the "big picture" using humans and their characteristics as the focal point. Once you have this framework of facts and assumptions you can then combine your personal knowledge with structured approaches to resolve the problem. The tangible gains come in the form of better personnel decisions, better product design, increased sales, and customer satisfaction and relations.

It is first important for you to see yourself and your business situations in the relevant chapters. To this end, I start each chapter with a set of questions that you might be asking and interject examples that my co-workers, colleagues, and clients have found helpful. The examples intentionally involve commonplace systems in order to allow you to understand the main points and not be burdened with overly complex material. Once you have connected, then the ensuing guidelines and tools will make more sense. Discussions of complex systems, theory, techniques can be found throughout the human systems literature, and unless you intend to invest a great deal of effort to learn, they can be difficult to synthesize. I hope you will find this book as a pleasant contrast to other sources in its usability. Although I intended to avoid overly scientific discussion, I found it impossible to include the necessary material without properly referencing originating sources.

Similarly, applied psychology students will find this book helpful for forming a general knowledge structure. This will serve as a framework for organizing the more detailed techniques and research information you will acquire throughout your education. From this, you too will develop a set of approaches to use in your own work. Secondly, throughout your career you will struggle to explain your field of study and career. Your set of skills do not likely fit into a specific job title. I have found one of the most effective ways is to describe an anecdotal project that the person can relate to. You may find some of the examples in this book helpful to use as explanations or for eliciting your own.

The major chapters are organized by four major groups of problems, which can be aided by having a better understanding of human abilities, personality, and behavior. The first two, personnel and training, share a commonality in the fact that they both are related to people's performance in the workplace. The third and fourth, technology insertion and interface design, and systems engineering are also closely connected in that they relate to people's performance using machines. Together, these pieces form a comprehensive business puzzle that applies to nearly everyone in the workforce.

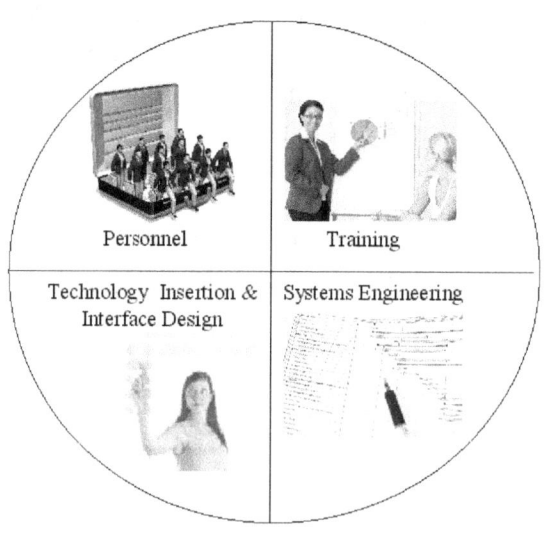

- **✚** The chapter on <u>personnel</u> includes the set of issues that pertain to performance in the workplace. This chapter is first for a few reasons. First, I consider it to be the lowest common denominator of all other business problems. Not only is it critical for things like selecting and placing employees, but it is also a common thread underlying the way people learn and use systems. Also, despite the recent increase in personal testing, the potential in this area is still underutilized. Second, this topic requires the discussion of how to decompose human characteristics into various taxonomies and it is most logical to discuss this first.
- **✚** The <u>training and expertise</u> chapter examines the idea of expertise and addresses ways for facilitating it. I have intentionally left the larger topic of *how* to develop training up to other available books.
- **✚** The chapter on <u>interface design</u> presents some rich examples of everyday systems and provides a deeper perspective of automation and design issues. I think you will find the discussion engaging and thought provoking.
- **✚** Finally, although <u>systems engineering</u> is not a business problem in itself, the process can greatly benefit from the human-centered approaches discussed herein. A human-centered approach will not necessarily be the only approach, and indeed should be used in complement with other approaches. Thus, the ideas expressed in the training and expertise chapter should be combined with recognized instructional system design (ISD) concepts; the interface design and systems engineering tools should be combined with established systems engineering practices.

Puzzle Piece 1: Personnel

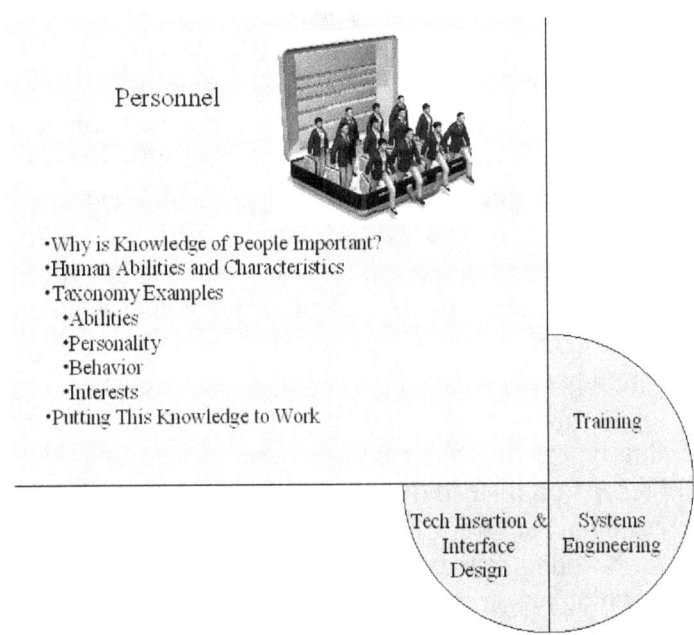

As a business owner or manager, you may be searching for solutions to the following personnel-related questions:

- ♣ Is our interviewing process performing well?
- ♣ How can we better understand the individual nature of our employees and candidates?
- ♣ What specific abilities are most critical for successful performance in this job?
- ♣ How can we hire the "right" employees?
- ♣ How should we place employees so that they will enjoy work and be motivated?

A common mantra found in company strategic plans and promotional materials is that "Our people are our greatest asset". While this is a noble statement and may indeed be true, the question that arises when I see this statement is "So what does this company do to make sure they hire, retain, and develop these assets?" And the answer is usually "nothing extraordinary". They have an interview process to screen new hires, conduct annual performance reviews, provide training, and even institute a vesting schedule to encourage people to wait for their retirement accounts to mature. These strategies all work to some degree, but fail in one way – they do not take into account an individual's personal characteristics to give them the best chance at reaching their and the company's potential. Interviews largely attempt to match job requirements and people's experience and are notoriously unreliable due to interviewer biases and business needs. Annual reviews tend to be metric driven and are often approached with a sense of apprehension instead of an opportunity to strategize careers. Training is useful for knowledge building, but has limitations for building true expertise. Vesting schedules are effective in keeping employees to a certain point, but when the schedule ends the company holds no advantage over competitors. In this chapter we will explore some extraordinary things can you do with your workforce, simply by gaining a better understanding of the people you work with and hire.

Why is Knowledge of People Important to Personnel Processes?

The subject of hiring, retaining, and motivating people in the workforce is the perfect place to begin the discussion of human characteristics. It lends itself nicely to the various taxonomies that will be presented. And the benefits of doing these processes correctly are clear. It also puts forward a perfect example of a context where the benefit of human characteristics knowledge is universally acknowledged, but where implementation is rarely performed correctly. I've witnessed interviews where candidates were barely given time to speak and walked out without knowing what they would be doing on a daily basis. In others, managers have given interviewers instructions such as "we're hiring aggressively. Just make sure they are company material". In both these cases, the hiring company is setting themselves up for potential failure by treating employees as interchangeable parts. With a little know-how and investment they could be taking steps to ensure higher rates of new hires that remain happily employed.

In the following section, you will see how knowledge of a person's abilities and personal characteristics can greatly enhance your ability to answer the questions above. As a result, you will hire and manage employees who are more motivated and productive.

Personnel Selection

If your organization is like most, your hiring process probably involves the interviewee meeting with a human resources representative followed by a series of one-on-one interviews with people that they will be working for or with. There may or may not be a standard list of questions, and often the interviewers are not provided with training or given time to prepare. It is common for an interviewer to be reading the interviewees' resume for the first time during the interview and fabricating questions on the fly. The results of these interviews are a general conclusion as to whether the person has the experience to qualify for the job and judgment about whether they like the person (consciously or unconsciously). Indeed, research has shown interviews to be a fundamentally unreliable hiring practice.

If you are from an organization that does require some form of testing, great! Well, maybe. Often tests are administered without knowing whether it is the right test (analysis) and whether it really works (validation). One of my clients only recently began requiring a vision test for an occupation that required the employee to look at detailed images all day. Instead, they previously used an interview and a writing sample to base their hiring decisions.

I bring personnel selection into this book on abilities and characteristics because I feel that it is one of the most predictably effective applications of human measurement. And it is quite easy to understand why. We've all been through the process of trying to figure out what type of career to pursue. Most of us thrashed our way through good and bad jobs in the pursuit of experience and money. Some people drive down the path which will provide the highest income. Others are in jobs because of connections, short-term opportunities, or any number of reasons. But people who truly enjoy their work and who are most productive typically are in positions that fit them well. They are doing activities that they enjoy and thus are intrinsically motivated. Motivating with money or threats of job security is like throwing cups of gasoline on a fire. There is action short term, but in the long run there is psychological dissonance which exhibits itself in the forms of low productivity, dissatisfaction, stress, and turnover.

Motivation

In addition to matching work with interests, it is important to recognize that some people are simply more intrinsically motivated by nature. That is, the nature in which they approach work allows them to be motivated in more situations. In his book Good to Great, Collins (2001) reports the results of an empirical study of companies that went through a transition leading to "greatness", as defined by a set of stringent criteria. One of the main findings was that these companies did not begin with new strategic mission statements, but rather they "cleaned house" and began by focusing on obtaining executives and other employees who were self-disciplined and self-motivated. In essence, the problems of how to manage and motivate employees went away, and the focus shifted to productivity. In the case of changing missions, these employees were better equipped to adapt to new situations and goals. Since this was an ad hoc study and included a multitude of companies, determining who these desirable employees were was not done in any one manner. It is likely that they relied mainly on interviews to make an assessment. The good news for you is that there are valid, reliable, and cost-effective ways to measure attributes like self-initiative and self-confidence. Other writings dealing with organizational culture, such as a widely recognized model proposed by Denison propose that a company's mission and employee involvement are the two most significant contributors to success. In the case of involvement, it makes good sense to recruit people who are inclined to be involved (i.e., self-initiative) rather than spending corporate energy to motivate those that are less inclined.

What Personnel Selection Means to You, a Business Manager

If you own or manage a business, there may be no other more important factor than personnel selection for determining the business' success, and more importantly, your and other's quality of life at work. We've all witnessed people who seem unrealistically happy doing very ordinary work such as driving tour busses or being a night watchman. What often appears as an act or a function of company training is really the simple result of fitting the right person with the right type of work and working conditions. In other words, training your employees is fine and advisable, but it only makes sense to concentrate on those with disposition for that type of work. In this way, expected performance will occur more naturally, especially when the employee must work under stressful circumstances. It sounds so easy, but is simply just not done enough in practice. With advancements in vocational and personality testing, why is this so rarely done? A couple of reasons come to mind. First, although persons early in their career get vocational guidance, they may not understand the workplace or even themselves well enough to make long-term employment decisions. In addition, the twists and turns involving experience, opportunities, failures, and income chasing have the tendency to send even the most focused individuals on career tangents.

Second, job satisfaction is not always dependent on the type of work being performed, but may instead be a reflection of compatibility with the organization and work environment. Some people have strong (and unrecognized) preferences about the amount of structure, communication with management and co-workers, and company identity. This last type of preference is trickier to recognize and measure and thus often overlooked. Self-recognition of one's true preferences may only come after working in a variety of jobs and settings.

Third, it requires a non-trivial effort on the part of the hiring organization. To implement selection tests properly, one must conduct a job analysis to identify what (knowledge, skills, abilities, and other personal characteristics) KSAOs are important to job performance, acquire tests to measure them, invest the time and money necessary to test applicants, and establish policies and practices for using the resulting information in an appropriate manner. Depending on whether the test scores are intended to be used as formal cut-offs to employment or as an interviewing aid, certain statistical tests are needed to show evidence of legality.

In response to the last reason, think about how much havoc one person can cause in a work group. An unsatisfied worker starts by mumbling behind the scenes, slowly discoloring the attitudes of others. As time goes on they become more vocal or isolated, and eventually can cause the need for managerial action or may leave the group, leaving rumors and bad feelings in their wake. Manager and employee time can be consumed by dealing formally and informally with this person. An extreme example of how this plays out can be seen on professional athletic teams. I have had the fortune of working with a group of talented researchers who provide personnel selection services to a host of National Football League teams. Through innovative questioning techniques and rigorous attention to scientific detail, they have developed valid methods for assessing a player's prospects on several dimensions, including the potential for getting into trouble both on and off the field. In light of the league's recent tough stance policy on criminal behavior, teams armed with this information have a low-cost way of reducing the risk of salary expenditures, draft picks, and team morale.

Round Pegs and Round Holes – Matching People and Jobs

Matching people to jobs is easier said than done. There are obvious abilities that point to certain jobs; people with athletic ability become athletes or trainers, people who are good at mathematics become various types of scientists, etc. But in other types of work it is not always easy to determine the best fit. Jobs are often broken down by the activities that are required, not the KSAOs that would lead to better performance. Even if KSAOs are defined, they are not likely to be tested, leaving it up to the discretion of an interviewer/interviewee meeting. And to make matters worse, the person may not understand themselves enough to know whether they are interested in the work.

I recall meeting with my high school career counselor before entering college. She oriented me on different collegiate and career paths. The one piece of advice she gave me was to "NEVER take a statistics course. The problems spread across 4 to 5 pages". I was pretty convinced by her fearful expression and was reluctant to take that step. In another instance, I remember pre-interviewing for an actuary position while in graduate school. I was taking statistics courses and figured this could be a possible path that I could pursue once out of school. Not more than a minute into the conversation, the woman on phone blurted "Are you sure you want this job? It is very boring". In hindsight, having made part of my living as a statistician, she was assuming I was just like her. But each person is very different when it comes to abilities, personality, and preferences. And that's good. Some people love doing jobs that others would find unpalatable. Borrowing a line from the movie Caddyshack, "The world needs ditch diggers too, Danny." And some people do prefer to dig ditches over wearing a suit and tie.

Another mistake that occurs is that groups focus on positive-only characteristics. While it is hard to imagine that we would desire negative aspects in a job, there are certain job types such as salespersons and positions of leadership where attributes that we consider negative can actually lead to greater success. Success in these positions often requires traits and dedication that lead to unbalanced lives. As pointed out by Smith (2007) a huge industry centers on the development of leadership. He makes the argument that the business of leadership development has taken the approach of building positive traits, but in actuality successful leaders possess several "taboo" traits. These include being less than honest to get what they want, internally justifying special treatment, and playing favorites. These can be assessed through personality and biodata measures such as persuasiveness, dedication, and integrity.

The key to understanding human abilities and characteristics is two-fold. First, we want to make sure the right people are hired and placed according to characteristics of the job. Second, by knowing what types of activities intrinsically motivate people, we can organize teams of people and define a division of labor that produces extraordinary results. We can let the extroverts network, people who prefer structure organize, analytical thinkers analyze, and so on. Again, this sounds intuitive, but it is rarely practiced due to a lack of awareness, know-how, and because it requires effort beyond the tactical here-and-now. There are reasonably priced commercial products that can aid you in this area. When researching them, it is important to note that some focus on abilities, some on work preferences, and others on behavioral tendencies. Your needs will determine the appropriateness of each. Most take the approach of quantitatively summarizing the person by using several dimensional continuums, such as preferences for the amount of information structure, making decisions based on evidence or beliefs, initiating new or maintaining on-going activities, and the amount of personal interaction.

<u>So, What About Interviews?</u>

You may be still wondering why it is so difficult to assess interviewees by way of an interview. Interviewees are coming into the interview with their best face. They may or may not be desperate for the job. They have time to acquire information about the company and job, and to prepare answers to questions they can anticipate. Combine that with non-standard interview processes and demonstrated personal biases, it is no wonder the interview process is so unreliable. It survives based on two things: people rely most on information they can physically see, and most importantly are overconfident about their own judgments.

Let me step back a moment and clarify that I'm not making the case for eliminating interviews from the selection process, especially if they are structured. It is entirely possible to detect someone that you know will not fit into the work group culture through discussion. I'm making the case that you should have more information tools than a resume in front of you when you perform the interview. Picture this: In addition to a resume, you carry a profile that describes the abilities and personal characteristics that lead to better performance in the target job. A rating associated with the interviewee accompanies each aspect as well as an overall rating on job fit. Furthermore, there is a list of questions that address noteworthy aspects. These questions help to enhance and standardize the interview group's approach.

Pulling these ideas together, the "products" that interview teams and managers need can be boiled down to:

1. A job analysis that indicates the important knowledge, skills, abilities, and other personal characteristics (personality, behavioral traits) that are important to perform the job and motivate the employee.
2. Tests for ascertaining these characteristics. Tests must be valid, reliable, and crafted to prevent faking.
3. An interview aid to address interviewee characteristics in relation to the job of interest. This will not only improve the validity of the questions asked, but will also increase reliability of the interviewer conclusions since they are using a consistent and valid approach.
4. An aid to form high-performing work groups. These can be used in several ways, although the basic idea is to create a division of labor whereby individuals are able to contribute by performing activities that they are naturally motivated to do. In both small working groups and larger programs managers can match personnel interests with tasks.

If all this sounds a little underhanded, take comfort in the fact that there are several positive outcomes of these types of tests. First, you are doing yourself a favor. If you are in an organization that truly cares about performance or quality of service, you must select the right people for the job. Even one person who is out of place can destroy the office social environment and create endless distractions for management. And don't dismiss the cost of turnover, which equals approximately 25% of an employee's salary (Employment Policy Foundation, 2004). Given that the overall private-sector average turnover rate is 25.1%, and 90% of these are voluntary quits, there is a large margin for improvement.

Second, you are doing the applicant a favor. As much as it hurts to be rejected, it is beneficial for someone to avoid being led along a path that will be unfavorable. Think about how it would be if our higher educational systems had no checkpoints, and instead let students take more and more classes of a subject they did not have the abilities to succeed in. The result would be people going through the motions of obtaining degrees with little or no guidance – only based on interest (yes, there is some of that anyways). In this case, you are avoiding placing a person who is not likely to be successful in the type of work involved.

Moving beyond the selection and placement process, you can use this knowledge to enhance the careers of those you do select. By knowing a person's strengths and weaknesses, you can select people with potential and remediate weaknesses through training, experiences, and mentoring. Most companies make claims that there most prized asset is their people and subscribe to the notion of mentoring. But let's be frank; most companies do little to nothing effective to enhance their people. Most managers are really administrators of budgets, plans, and schedules, and there is little reward for them to do personnel management. These activities are more visible and verifiable to upper management. Personnel development is often transparent, only revealing itself over time in the form of culture and turnover statistics.

Defining Human Abilities and Characteristics

There are a wide variety of KSAOs. Fortunately, it isn't likely that you will have to consider many in a given context, but you will almost always be served by considering something. Often it will not be a matter of having to identify and measure specific aspects. Rather, in some cases it is enough to scope the problem at hand and characterize the user groups so as to be able to anticipate requirements, risks, exceptions, or other knowledge that leads to better understanding of what you are dealing with.

Before launching into the various sets of abilities and characteristics, I'll answer the first question that is probably going through your mind, that being "Is there any one thing that best predicts performance on the job?" The answer is surprisingly "Yes", and of course "It depends". The "Yes" answer is based on a review of thousands of research studies conducted over 85 years in which Schmidt and Hunter (1998) concluded that general mental ability (GMA) or intelligence is the best predictor of future job performance, and in particular for professional-managerial and high complexity jobs. Intelligence in this case refers to the ability to reason, as opposed to knowledge learned through education. The logic behind this is easy to comprehend. Performance is highly dependent on a person's ability to grasp the scope of what they are doing, acquire new knowledge, make decisions based on information and reasoning, direct actions toward productive ends, and adapt to exceptional circumstances. This extends past the task at hand to their life state of affairs in general.

The "It depends" answer acknowledges the fact that several other general and job-specific abilities should be considered in combination with intelligence. Schmidt and Hunter (1998) reported the amount of incremental validity (i.e., predictability) provided by various assessment methods and personal characteristics in addition to intelligence. The best methods to apply were a combination of GMA and a work sample test and GMA and structured interviews. Both of these methods have some trade-offs. Work samples may be costly to produce and are only relevant for assessing persons with assumed experience. They require extensive analysis to develop measures that predict performance. This may include the construction of specialized assessment settings such as simulators. Thus, they are often used for assessing people entering skilled trade positions or inherently risky positions. Interviews are effective when they are structured, but less so when unstructured. Structured interviewing requires developing sets of questions that are predictors of good performance. These must be asked in the same manner by all interviewers in order to provide comparable responses. Interviews in most corporate settings, where interviewees are passed through multiple interview discussions would fall under the unstructured category. The third combination includes the combination of GMA with the personal trait "integrity". As we shall discuss below, integrity is itself is a combination of personality and behavioral characteristics.

The second question that you are probably asking at this point is what kind of results you can expect if implementing these methods. The best answer would be fairly good, but keep in mind that any predictions are probabilistic. Going back to Schmidt and Hunter's (1998) results, the best validity combinations result in validity in the .55 - .60 region (validity ranges from a 0 to a perfect 1.0). Although this appears moderate and stresses the fact that there will be some predictive "mistakes", it is actually quite impressive as research goes. They point out that in research reporting employee performance in terms of output, variability between employees is quite high, adding to the importance of using valid selection procedures.

Examples of Taxonomies

The first step toward implementing a testing or research plan involving human characteristics is to understand the fundamental aspects that make up an individual. It is all about understanding that there are individual differences between humans; everyone has strengths and weaknesses. We all know people have abilities and personality, but what about the lower level aspects? Is there any agreed upon set of characteristic measures to choose from? The truth is that there are no universal solutions, as many schemes exist. However, there has been much work in this field, and there are schemes that are recognized, as you will soon see.

The aim is to identify sets of characteristics, whether physical, personality, perceptual, or behavioral that are close to being comprehensive and mutually exclusive. The type of characteristic you consider will be dependent on the persons and tasks of interest. In most cases, you will narrow the focus to include just a relevant range of factors. In other words, different types of characteristics will be chosen based on different types of job and task settings. If this selection has any legal implications or needs a theoretical justification, it should be based on a systematic job or task analysis.

As mentioned earlier, the commonly used acronym KSAOs stands for knowledge, skills, abilities, and other personal characteristics. Knowledge is the information that one obtains through experience and education. Since they are often confused, it is important to make a distinction between abilities and skills. Abilities are an inherent and enduring characteristic, while skills are a learned capacity. In general, a person's full potential is a product of the inherent ability combined with the amount of effort placed in skill development. For example, a person has a certain level of athletic ability and develops specific athletic skills, such as hitting a baseball through training and practice. Someone with a low level of athleticism will probably attain only moderate performance despite large levels of training. On the other hand, an athletically gifted person will probably not reach full potential without some amount of training. In the past, KSAs were all most organizations focused on for personnel selection. Over the past few decades, we have come to realize the importance of other personal characteristics, most notably personality, past behavior, and interests – thus the 'O' in KSAO. The following sections will make clear the next level of detail each of these characteristics.

Abilities

The O*NET-SOC system (visit at http://online.onetcenter.org) is the nation's primary standard for occupational classification (SOC), recently replacing the longstanding Dictionary of Occupational Titles (DOT). The Office of Management and Budget (OMB) has mandated the use of this classification system for all federal agencies that collect and disseminate occupational information. The O*NET^{T}database contains information on hundreds of standardized and occupation-specific descriptors. It is based heavily on decades of human ability research by Fleishman and others (Fleishman & Mumford (1991); Fleishman & Reilly (1992)), which evolved in form from the Manual for the Ability Requirements Scale (MARS) to the Fleishman Job Analysis Survey (F-JAS) and finally to O*NET™ (Peterson, et al., 1997). Although there is debate over the methodology used to produce the O*Net reliability and validity ratings (Harvey and Hollender, 2002), it is useful for understanding the spectrum KSAOs that make up various jobs. The website allows you to either examine the underlying KSAOs associated with a job title or search for job titles associated with particular KSAOs. O*NET explicitly uses the knowledge, skills, and abilities titles, but also includes work activities, interests, and work values. It is important to note that some of the underlying factors are treated differently under other taxonomy schemes. For instance, some of the social skills listed overlap with definitions within personality schemes, as we will see. General intelligence also will account for some aspects related to things like complex problem solving and critical thinking, which O*NET includes as skills.

For our purpose, I'll introduce the O*NET™ scales for abilities, and use other examples for personality and behavior. The O*NET descriptors include 52 scales to rate ability constructs, organized under the cognitive, physical, psychomotor, and sensory groupings. As you read through each set of abilities, keep in mind that the intention is to define the lowest level set of distinct abilities. The physical abilities are listed first as they are easier to visualize relative to the cognitive abilities.

Physical Abilities	Abilities that influence strength, endurance, flexibility, balance and coordination
Dynamic Flexibility	The ability to quickly and repeatedly bend, stretch, twist, or reach out with your body, arms, and/or legs.
Dynamic Strength	The ability to exert muscle force repeatedly or continuously over time. This involves muscular endurance and resistance to muscle fatigue.
Explosive Strength	The ability to use short bursts of muscle force to propel oneself (as in jumping or sprinting), or to throw an object.

Extent Flexibility	The ability to bend, stretch, twist, or reach with your body, arms, and/or legs.
Gross Body Coordination	The ability to coordinate the movement of your arms, legs, and torso together when the whole body is in motion.
Gross Body Equilibrium	The ability to keep or regain your body balance or stay upright when in an unstable position.
Stamina	The ability to exert yourself physically over long periods of time without getting winded or out of breath.
Static Strength	The ability to exert maximum muscle force to lift, push, pull, or carry objects.
Trunk Strength	The ability to use your abdominal and lower back muscles to support part of the body repeatedly or continuously over time without 'giving out' or fatiguing.

Psychomotor Abilities	Abilities that influence the capacity to manipulate and control objects
Arm-Hand Steadiness	The ability to keep your hand and arm steady while moving your arm or while holding your arm and hand in one position.
Control Precision	The ability to quickly and repeatedly adjust the controls of a machine or a vehicle to exact positions.
Finger Dexterity	The ability to make precisely coordinated movements of the fingers of one or both hands to grasp, manipulate, or assemble very small objects.
Manual Dexterity	The ability to quickly move your hand, your hand together with your arm, or your two hands to grasp, manipulate, or assemble objects.
Multilimb Coordination	The ability to coordinate two or more limbs (for example, two arms, two legs, or one leg and one arm) while sitting, standing, or lying down. It does not involve performing the activities while the whole body is in motion.
Rate Control	The ability to time your movements or the movement of a piece of equipment in anticipation of changes in the speed and/or direction of a moving object or scene.
Reaction Time	The ability to quickly respond (with the hand, finger, or foot) to a signal (sound, light, picture) when it appears.

Response Orientation	The ability to choose quickly between two or more movements in response to two or more different signals (lights, sounds, pictures). It includes the speed with which the correct response is started with the hand, foot, or other body part.
Speed of Limb Movement	The ability to quickly move the arms and legs.
Wrist-Finger Speed	The ability to make fast, simple, repeated movements of the fingers, hands, and wrists.

Cognitive Abilities	Abilities that influence the acquisition and application of knowledge in problem solving
Category Flexibility	The ability to generate or use different sets of rules for combining or grouping things in different ways.
Deductive Reasoning	The ability to apply general rules to specific problems to produce answers that make sense.
Flexibility of Closure	The ability to identify or detect a known pattern (a figure, object, word, or sound) that is hidden in other distracting material.
Fluency of Ideas	The ability to come up with a number of ideas about a topic (the number of ideas is important, not their quality, correctness, or creativity).
Inductive Reasoning	The ability to combine pieces of information to form general rules or conclusions (includes finding a relationship among seemingly unrelated events).
Information Ordering	The ability to arrange things or actions in a certain order or pattern according to a specific rule or set of rules (e.g., patterns of numbers, letters, words, pictures, mathematical operations).
Mathematical Reasoning	The ability to choose the right mathematical methods or formulas to solve a problem.
Memorization	The ability to remember information such as words, numbers, pictures, and procedures.
Number Facility	The ability to add, subtract, multiply, or divide quickly and correctly.
Oral Comprehension	The ability to listen to and understand information and ideas presented through spoken words and sentences.
Oral Expression	The ability to communicate information and ideas in speaking so others will understand.

Originality	The ability to come up with unusual or clever ideas about a given topic or situation, or to develop creative ways to solve a problem.
Perceptual Speed	The ability to quickly and accurately compare similarities and differences among sets of letters, numbers, objects, pictures, or patterns. The things to be compared may be presented at the same time or one after the other. This ability also includes comparing a presented object with a remembered object.
Problem Sensitivity	The ability to tell when something is wrong or is likely to go wrong. It does not involve solving the problem, only recognizing there is a problem.
Selective Attention	The ability to concentrate on a task over a period of time without being distracted.
Spatial Orientation	The ability to know your location in relation to the environment or to know where other objects are in relation to you.
Speed of Closure	The ability to quickly make sense of, combine, and organize information into meaningful patterns.
Time Sharing	The ability to shift back and forth between two or more activities or sources of information (such as speech, sounds, touch, or other sources).
Visualization	The ability to imagine how something will look after it is moved around or when its parts are moved or rearranged.
Written Comprehension	The ability to read and understand information and ideas presented in writing.
Written Expression	The ability to communicate information and ideas in writing so others will understand.

Sensory Abilities	Abilities that influence visual, auditory and speech perception
Auditory Attention	The ability to focus on a single source of sound in the presence of other distracting sounds.
Depth Perception	The ability to judge which of several objects is closer or farther away from you, or to judge the distance between you and an object.
Far Vision	The ability to see details at a distance.
Glare Sensitivity	The ability to see objects in the presence of glare or bright lighting.

Hearing Sensitivity	The ability to detect or tell the differences between sounds that vary in pitch and loudness.
Near Vision	The ability to see details at close range (within a few feet of the observer).
Night Vision	The ability to see under low light conditions.
Peripheral Vision	The ability to see objects or movement of objects to one's side when the eyes are looking ahead.
Sound Localization	The ability to tell the direction from which a sound originated.
Speech Clarity	The ability to speak clearly so others can understand you.
Speech Recognition	The ability to identify and understand the speech of another person.
Visual Color Discrimination	The ability to match or detect differences between colors, including shades of color and brightness.

A second cognitive ability taxonomy worthy of mention, along with a kit containing paper and pencil tests, was published in 1976 by Eckstrom, et al. while at the Educational Testing Service. Many of the factors are shared with the scheme above, so it is not worth repeating here. Again, the factors and associated definitions describe a comprehensive view of cognition, and the accompanying tests help to illustrate the operational meaning. These tests may only be used in research settings; however, other researchers have used them as a basis for creating validated computer-based versions.

Personality

In addition to abilities that are relevant to the job, personality is a significant consideration for a person's fit in a line of work. And with abilities, there are no one-size-fits-all answers. Upon inspection of various personality traits, we can however paint a general picture of the jobs and people that fit together well.

The table below lists one way of breaking down personality into components. In this case, I have used the labels from what is widely accepted as the "big 5" factors (source: scientific consensus) and interspersed them with sub-factors as described by Saucier and Ostendorf (1999). Upon examination, it is easy to see why these play an important role in how individuals succeed or not in various careers and work roles.

Big Five Factor	Sub-factors
1) Extraversion	
	a) Sociability (sociable, cheerful, merry, effervescent)
	b) Unrestraint (talkative, verbal, aggressive, domineering)
	c) Assertiveness (assertive, straightforward, direct, bold)
	d) Activity-adventurousness (daring, adventurous, active, competitive, rambunctious)
2) Agreeableness	
	a) Warmth-affection (affectionate, sentimental, sensitive, warm)
	b) Gentleness (agreeable, cordial, amiable)
	c) Generosity (charitable, helpful, generous, unselfish)
	d) Modesty-humility (modest, humble)
3) Conscientiousness	
	a) Orderliness (organized, orderly, neat, meticulous)
	b) Decisiveness-consistency (decisive, firm, consistent, steady)
	c) Reliability (reliable, dependable, responsible, prompt, punctual, respectful)
	d) Industriousness (ambitious, industrious, purposeful, conscientious)
4) Emotional Stability	
	a) Irritability (undemanding, uncritical, tranquil)
	b) Insecurity (relaxed, unenvious)
	c) Emotionality (unemotional, unexcitable)
5) Intellect-Imagination	
	a) Intellect (intelligent, intellectual, philosophical, analytical, knowledgeable, complex)
	b) Imagination-creativity (creative, inventive, imaginative, artistic, clever, innovative)
	c) Perceptiveness (perceptive, insightful, foresighted)

In the case of extraversion, or put another way an introversion-extraversion continuum, being extraverted is advantageous on several fronts. Sociability provides a natural tendency to establish networks, important for information sharing and making positive impressions. Assertiveness helps to exude a sense of confidence and can be helpful for communication and negotiation. Extraverts are motivated to perform jobs in sales, health care, and customer service. However, it is important to understand when particular jobs might be better served by people with introverted tendencies. Jobs requiring a person to concentrate for long periods of time, such as technicians, investigators, and scientists provide intrinsic satisfaction to introverts, while creating boredom for extraverts.

Agreeableness comes into play in several job categories. People who are sensitive and gentle work well in customer service and health care professions. Interestingly, generosity is a valuable characteristic for companies to recruit, as it is an important attribute for those that will become good mentors.

Conscientiousness is the best single personality predictor of performance across job types behind general intelligence. Persons high on this trait work with purpose. They work well with others due to their predictable nature, and provide and accept feedback. They tend to take initiative and identify opportunities to acquire new skills. The larger construct, integrity (as measured by commercial integrity tests) has been found to a large extent to be a measure of conscientiousness, with some overlap with agreeableness and emotional stability.

Emotional stability speaks largely for itself. Those that can take the ups and downs at the workplace are more likely to prosper. This becomes even more significant at higher level positions where more difficult issues and debate must be dealt with.
Finally, intellect and imagination, as well as having genuine interest in the job type, are important for high performing individuals. These people develop transferable skills and are able

to apply them creatively to new settings. They have the foresight to understand co-worker and client needs and prepare accordingly.

Behavior

In the context of personnel selection, we are interested in behavior as a set of past experiences that can serve as predictors of future behavior. Indeed, it makes logical sense that this would be the best way to base predictions. As we have just seen, previous researchers have provided helpful taxonomic schemes to describe sets of abilities and personality traits. Unfortunately, there is no similar taxonomy for behaviors. Whereas abilities and personality are inherent and fairly stable traits, behavior is a somewhat open-ended set of outcomes reflecting a combination of personal traits and responses to situational, environmental, and social factors. An example is the tendencies of a person making decisions under time stress. In this case the person's abilities and personality traits combine to produce an outcome that usually shows a consistent bias over time and similar circumstances. The resulting behaviors are more global than the underlying ability and personality traits. Thus, researchers have had to fabricate constructs that make sense in the context of interest.

So what behavioral constructs might be relevant to good job performance? Some predictors that span across many jobs include:
- Integrity: Predictor of job performance as well as identifying people who are likely to exhibit illegal and counterproductive behaviors.
- Dedication: Reflects the willingness to work toward goals. This is especially critical if the job requires a great amount career investment in the way of education and training.
- Self-confidence: Examines the feeling that a person will be able to successfully cope with current and future demands and problems.
- Intrinsic motivation: Reflects that the person derives satisfaction from performing internally, rather than needing

approval from others. These people tend to be self-initiators.

Other behaviors will reflect the specific needs of study. As an example, a proposed study targeting commercial vehicle driver safety includes medical factors as well as personality and behavioral factors believed to have meaningful relationships to accidents and violations. The specific factors include: energy level, driver anger, attentional focus, machoism, boredom propensity, and stress under time pressure. These can be assessed through self-reporting questionnaires or through reports from valid observers.

One obvious hurdle to overcome when assessing self-reported behaviors is a bias toward giving socially acceptable responses. It is a natural defense mechanism for people to paint themselves in a good light. So, how can we rely on anything that is self-reported? Fortunately, recent questioning techniques have led to improved ways to prevent response bias and faking.

Interests
Among Schmidt and Hunter's (1998) findings, interests had very little predictive value for job performance. Their rationale is that interests influence which jobs people pursue, but once they are in the job, intelligence and personality traits determine performance. To that conclusion I would offer that interests may be more important in predicting job satisfaction, which in turn affects tenure and general demeanor on the job. The point is that performance is not the only important determiner of job success. Work preferences, as described earlier, follow this same logic. Although people are adaptive and can survive in suboptimal situations, they are more likely to thrive in optimal situations.

Putting This Knowledge to Use

To make this discussion a little more concrete, let's look at an example of research that exemplifies the decomposition of tasks, identification of relevant abilities and personal characteristics, and measurement. To obtain a driver's license one must complete a written knowledge test, take a driving test, and most states pass a test for static visual acuity (i.e., the ability to see a non-moving object with some defined degree of clarity). Static visual acuity is checked by all states before obtaining a license due to its ease of measurement and belief that it is important to driver safety. What isn't known, however, is how valid this test is. Research has shown static visual acuity to have small, but significant correlation to traffic accidents in some studies (Burg, 1967), but no significant relationship in others (Henderson and Burg, 1973). Now, I'm all for people knowing rules, being able to see, and demonstrating that they can drive before getting on the road, but we shouldn't have false confidence that by measuring static acuity we are making the roads much safer. Clearly there are a lot of things happening that require more than being able to identify static objects.

Let's give the benefit of a doubt to the usefulness of the written and driving tests and examine abilities that relate to driving performance. Before doing so, I must caveat this discussion by alluding to the fact that predicting accident rates from ability variables is quite difficult and probabilistic. Accidents are infrequent events that are not always defined in the same way or reported, and may be a result of multiple factors, many of which will not be documented or known. For these reasons, using accident data to understand the intricacies of human performance issues has not been overly successful.

Depending on your objective the taxonomies explored above may suit your needs without modification. In other cases flexibility may be needed to accommodate your intent or to conform to existing research. In an extensive literature review we (Barnes, Llaneras, Brock, and Swezey, 1994) summarized past research

30

related to abilities and driving performance, particularly that which was related to older drivers. We used a taxonomy similar to what we have seen, but modified it by reducing the number of abilities to those that are relevant to driving and by expanding the number of visual abilities. This was influenced by the specialization inherent in the research. Note that as the amount of specialization increased, abilities became less mutually exclusive (e.g., Useful field of vision is a combination of attention and visual abilities).

The resulting taxonomies in our review were:

Cognitive Abilities
- Decision-making – The ability to tell when a situation requires action and to take appropriate action.
- Selective attention – The ability to concentrate on a task one is doing.
- Attention sharing – The ability to shift back and forth between two or more sources of information.

Perceptual Abilities
- Static visual acuity – The ability to resolve details of a stationary target.
- Dynamic visual acuity – The ability to resolve details of a moving target.
- Contrast sensitivity – The ability to detect targets of varying contrast.
- Useful field of vision – The area of the visual field that is useful for acquiring information during a brief glance.
- Field dependence – The ability to perceive relevant targets embedded within a complex scene.
- Depth perception – The ability to judge distance, and changes in distance, from an object moving either laterally or longitudinally.
- Glare sensitivity – The ability to detect stimuli in the visual field in the presence of extremely bright illumination.

- Night vision – The ability to perform visual functions under dim illumination levels.
- Audition – The ability to detect and discriminate among sounds that vary over broad ranges of frequency or amplitude.

Psychomotor Abilities
- Reaction time
- Multilimb coordination
- Control precision

The practical application lies in establishing ability to performance correlations, and establishing testing policies, such as those for hiring or for obtaining driver licenses. On-going research is attempting to identify statistical evidence of links between abilities such as these and a more extreme case of driving – that of a commercial vehicle. The added weight and size of these vehicles places strain on a driver, requiring greater use of perceptual, cognitive, and physical abilities. Drivers must control larger and heavier vehicles under more extreme conditions since they don't always have the flexibility of when they drive. Routine activities such as accelerating on ramps and making turns at intersection become significantly more difficult in a commercial vehicle, taxing resources needed to see in dynamic visual settings, coordinate physical movements, attend to multiple circumstances, and make decisions. In addition, the consequence of accidents is much greater. This leads to the conclusion that it might be worth performing more stringent testing as part of the licensing requirement for commercial drivers.

Measuring Human Characteristics

In some cases, it may be enough to identify important KSAOs and either be aware of them or consider them in a general sense. However, identification may be only half the battle in cases where measurement is needed. Measurements take many forms and there is a continuum of ease of measurement depending on the amount of invasiveness required to measure. On one end are biographical data such as age, height, and weight that can be easily captured verbally or through surveys. Somewhere in the middle are normative data, such as anthropometric data and cognitive ability studies which can be researched or purchased. A notable trend brought about by computing power and improved human measurements such as by the Civilian American and European Surface Anthropometry Resource Project (CAESAR) is the use of digital human models. These can be used in design to improve survivability and hospitability of warfighting environments, ship and other close quarter design, clothing design, and job selection in situations where size and mobility are critical. Most invasive are measures that must be taken through direct sampling. In this case, tests must be acquired, individuals must be recruited, and testing must be conducted. An added complication with this type of testing in academic and government settings is that sampling plans must be approved by institutional review boards.

The market for measurement tools can be characterized as a cottage industry; the simple explanation being that the markets for these products is small. Individual researchers will often attempt to sell tools that they have developed and found useful. In the case of larger markets, such as intelligence, school psychometrics, and personality testing, sales volume may be great enough to support a small company. Some of these tests have become commonplace and have gained name recognition, for better or worse.

As with any shopping experience, it is difficult as a consumer to decipher the product's capabilities and characteristics and make decisions about what test to use. Three specific things to consider when surveying tests are validity, reliability, and nature of relationship of what you are measuring to performance. Unlike physical products, these characteristics are abstract and easy to overlook.

Validity refers to the extent to which the tool is measuring what it is intended to measure. Establishing validity is difficult for a number of reasons. By the nature of measuring something with a second tool, especially in a naturalistic setting, there will almost always be a less than perfect measurement. In the case of cognitive testing, there is also an issue of defining what is being measured. If you take the time to delve into the literature surrounding cognitive abilities, you will see an endless debate about whether tests are measuring the intended ability or something else. In some cases it is an issue with the measuring tool and in other cases it is a labeling issue. The previously mentioned cognitive test kit (Eckstrom, et. al.) contains good objective background discussions surrounding each of their tests.

This debate has played out most visibly in relation to intelligence testing. Let's consider the Wonderlic intelligence test, which has gained name recognition, in large part due to its' recently mandated use in the NFL pre-draft assessments of prospective college football players. This test is composed of 50 multiple choice questions, and responders are given 12 minutes to answer as many as possible. The summary is given as a single score, which is claimed to measure general intelligence. But one has to question what this is really measuring and the relevance to the job of playing football. The biggest issues with this test is that it is largely biased due to its' dependence on reading comprehension ability and that there is little evidence suggesting a relationship with performance. It is unknown whether intelligence as measured by this test aids a player in learning playbooks or thinking on the field. The media has reported average scores by position, but it is not clear what importance this has in general, much less by position. Requiring players to take this test is a good example of test misuse and doing oneself a disservice, especially considering that there are better suited tests.

Reliability is the degree to which performance is consistent across measurements and time. Like validity, most measures' reliability will fall below perfection. Validity and reliability are most often reported on a 0 to 1 scale, where 1 is perfect. A good way to think of validity and reliability is by considering the analogy of a scale for measuring weight. Validity would reflect the scale's precision, while reliability would reflect variations. Thus, if a scale indicated that a 180 lb. man weighed 180.1 lbs., it would be considered to have high validity. If repeated measurements indicated that there was little variation despite changes in stance, then it would also be considered to have high reliability.

Personnel Recap

In this chapter we explored the importance of understanding employees as individuals who possess varying characteristics. We examined how you can build an interviewing toolkit and use information about interviewees to increase the likelihood that they will be motivated to work and perform well in the intended position. This information can likewise be used to better understand current employees and help build high performing teams.

Second, I unveiled several taxonomies dealing with physical, cognitive, and personality characteristics. These provide you with a structured way of identifying, testing, and expressing the various characteristics that may be important to jobs and tasks in your workplace. You will find this information as a helpful reference as we move on to explore the topics of training and technology insertion.

Key take-aways:
+ Hiring employees who are self-motivated and matched well with job characteristics may be the most important thing you can do toward creating a high performing organization
+ You can build an effective interview toolkit to improve the selection process.

♣ Taxonomies describing abilities and personality provide a useful way to assess a person's characteristics.

Puzzle Piece 2: Training and Expertise

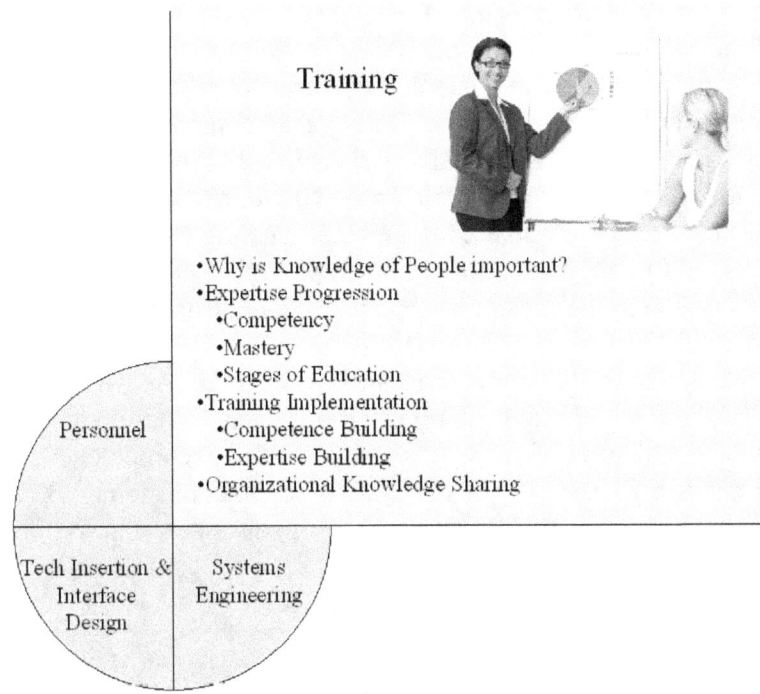

Training

- Why is Knowledge of People important?
- Expertise Progression
  - Competency
  - Mastery
  - Stages of Education
- Training Implementation
  - Competence Building
  - Expertise Building
- Organizational Knowledge Sharing

Personnel

Tech Insertion & Interface Design

Systems Engineering

As a business owner or manager, you may be searching for solutions to the following training questions:

- ✂ What competencies are needed to be able to perform this job?
- ✂ Can job requirements be taught (skills), or are they largely reliant on a person's inherent abilities?
- ✂ How do I adapt training to accommodate people's learning preferences?
- ✂ How can we become a "learning company"?

Why is Knowledge of People Important to Training?

The general aim of training is to bridge a gap between a trainee's current knowledge or skills and a target state needed to perform at some desired level. To accomplish this, the training organization conducts training needs analyses and constructs training modules to address the defined objectives. Recognized approaches, such as Instructional System Design (ISD), Criterion Referenced Instruction (CRI), and Performance-based Training (PBT) provide systematic guidance for analyzing and constructing training programs, and by all means should be employed. These systems share many commonalities, most notably the identification of training needs, the mastery of materials to knowledge and skill, and performance evaluation against success criteria. As we shall see shortly, implementing training programs such as these may lead to the acquisition of knowledge, skills, or even competency, but not necessarily the truly desired outcome – that of increased expertise.

Expertise Progression

Understanding how learning and expertise evolve provides strong insight for understanding the appropriate applications of training programs. Expertise, in general, can be further delineated into the concepts of <u>competence</u> and <u>mastery</u>. Competence, as used in professional circles, refers to a set of educational gates, experiences, and performance indicators that suggest a person has achieved a level of capability in a given area. These are usually achieved through standard processes and experiences, and are adequate for the everyday purposes associated with that competency. In actuality, most persons settle at some level of competence in one or more types of work (van Gelder, et. al., 2004). Competency is what we are realistically able to ascertain from resumes and interviews. Mastery, on the other hand, is characterized by a highly developed pattern of being able to combine previous knowledge and experiences to creatively solve difficult problems and generate new ideas.

Competency

Most organizations use a knowledge building approach to building employee competencies. It is convenient to think of knowledge as existing in two forms. On the simplest level, procedural knowledge consists of facts, rules, and basic concepts. This is the typical way students in a school environment are taught. As the term suggests, this knowledge helps understand how things work and at some level how to perform actions. Declarative knowledge goes beyond this rote form into fluid reasoning, interpretation, and strategic thinking. It is a foundation of knowledge and opinion structures that allow for higher-level judgments and problem solving. One way to think of declarative knowledge is that, once established, it allows someone to do an activity even if the procedural knowledge is forgotten. Imagine a novice who follows a cookbook to measure ingredients and perform procedures needed to complete a recipe. An expert cook would have developed enough reasoning skills to not only follow the recipe, but also improvise if forced to use some alternative ingredients or cooking techniques.

Mastery

Mastery represents a higher level of expertise characterized by a greater ability to apply reasoning in order to understand situations in greater depth or generalize skills to other problem sets. Novices tend to focus on singular facts and anecdotes, and fail to translate them into more general concepts and trends. In turn, they are less capable of applying critical analysis to available evidence and information. As a result, they form simpler solutions and are often overconfident in their decisions. Widespread evidence of this has been documented in studies of stock market trading. Novices fail to integrate the multitude of variables involved in stock selection and how that decision fits into the larger scheme of their portfolios and long-term strategy (if one exists). As a result of tunnel vision, they tend to take greater risks and be overconfident because they do not possess the sophistication to take different perspectives. Experts on the other hand are able to quickly discriminate and extract information, distinguish between salient and distracting information, and visualize trends and patterns. They are able to critique their performance and make future adjustments. We can witness this by observing doctors that can quickly scan x-rays, people who can mentally multiply 3-digit numbers, and experimental designers who can quickly determine appropriate statistical methods to apply.

Interestingly, experts may still have difficulty describing the procedures and knowledge they use to complete tasks and make decisions. Once an activity becomes ingrained or automated, the person tends to perform it without paying conscious attention to it. This is one of the challenges corporations face when expert workers retire. They may be willing to share experiences, but documenting them and storing them in usable form is no small feat, especially in the case of mental tasks. Experts must have enough insight to understand what they know and how to translate it into a meaningful presentation. The most commonly used technique is to write the information into prose, since it is most economical. However, on top of the translation problem, this requires the recipient to retrieve and read it at a later time. Bottom line: it just isn't effective. Cognitive task analyses, while useful for other types of investigations, are equally ineffective in a training endeavor.

Logically, there should be a correlation between years of experience and level of expertise, since someone with a longer work history is likely to have experienced more situations requiring intense study and problem solving. There is some truth to this, but it isn't a straight yardstick. Job experience has been shown to have a moderate correlation with job performance up to five years on the job, after which more experience results in increasingly smaller increments in performance (Schmidt, Hunter, and Outerbridge, 1986). Using the view of expertise just described makes it clear that it is entirely possible to have incongruence between a person's longevity and formal credentials (e.g., educational degree) and their ability to perform. I suspect that most of us hold this suspicion, but because it is difficult to quickly know a person's true level of expertise, we rely heavily on formal criteria such as degrees and grades. This is common and is illustrated by statistics showing poor validity and reliability when using credential criteria and interviewing techniques for job candidate selection. Hopefully this book has armed you with enough information to be able to craft some inquiring questions to ascertain whether a person can provide the precise services you need.

As mentioned above, we would like to be able to break down expertise into components in order to train them or automate them with computers. In practice, modeling expertise is difficult, due to the fact that the majority of everyday reasoning in the workforce can be considered to be informal. That is, people, and especially experts, process the information at hand by supplementing it with prior experiences, strategies, knowledge, and beliefs (Evans and Thompson, 2004). This flies in the face of what researchers would like to believe -- that expertise can be represented by formal knowledge and rule structures (i.e., if-then rules; "If this happens, then I do that"). Using formal logic enhances researcher's ability to contrive precise experimental settings. Under these controlled conditions participant performance can be compared to defined and quantified performance criteria. In the case of computers, which lend themselves to formal logic, this is quite appropriate. However, in the case of humans, this approach lacks validity, despite quantification that might suggest otherwise. What we as a scientific community end up with is an understanding that experts do use some formal logic, but that there are other factors that avoid capture.

Van Gelder, et al. (2004) have proposed that most people develop a certain level of informal reasoning or competence relative to their peers, but that people rarely advance beyond that to attain a genuine mastery of a given set of skills. Maturation and exposure to various experiences yields some improvement, but most people tend to settle into some stable state of "unfinished competence". And in a general sense this is understandable. Most people are not driven to be experts in one, much less multiple fields, whether it is through self-satisfaction or lack of determination. At a more molecular level, people do try to gain some level of expertise in something over the course of their lives. In this light, evidence shows that expertise develops only after very large amounts of practice consciously aimed at improvement, done in intense regular timeframes, using exercises that are progressively graduated, designed specifically to enhance particular aspects of performance, and are supervised or coached (including feedback). I would temper this with two moderating factors: that expertise is shaped by the individuals' underlying abilities and interests. Thus, someone may be willing to undergo training to learn how to mentally calculate numbers or use a keyboard, but unless they have some level of numerical reasoning or manual dexterity combined with interest, the skills will never fully develop. We indeed see the truth in this in the athletic arena where expertise is easily observed and measured under competition. We can witness examples where persons with high athletic ability excel in combination with good training practices. We can also see examples where performance falls short of this due to either lower levels of preparation or fundamental ability.

Although this view of expertise development makes sense, it is not good news for those in academic or corporate personal development arenas, where it is simply not feasible to dedicate this level of attention and training to individuals. So what are we as educators and human development personnel to do? The best approach is to develop an understanding of the levels of educational accomplishment and determine which of these fits your realistic organizational needs. You can then match the best implementation strategies for making your training purpose-appropriate and economical. Again, previous research provides tools to accomplish this.

Stages of Education

Blooms taxonomy provides a simple overview of the hierarchical stages of education (Bloom, 1956). Each stage represents a distinct level of sophistication related to the ability to grasp and use information. While we would ideally like to create a training environment that propels students to the highest level of education, this is not practical in most situations. As you read each of these descriptions, ascertain which level most of your training realistically targets.

Knowledge: Acquiring terminology, specific facts, universals, and abstractions in a field. Learning at this level is measured by the extent to which this material can be reproduced.

Comprehension: Understanding the meaning of informational materials. This is in general the level of education that is produced by schools and corporations. Students passively attend to lectures, classroom activities, or textbooks. The instructor attempts to maintain attention and convey a set of facts and concepts. Interaction is mostly done through question and answering and perhaps some defined activities.

Application: Using previously learned information in new and concrete situations to solve problems that have single or best answers. In school settings this is typically developed through drill-and-practice techniques. Corporate training often attempts to achieve this level of learning by using participative problem-solving using assumed student knowledge.

Analysis: Breaking down informational materials into their component parts, examining such information to develop divergent conclusions by identifying motives or causes, making inferences, and/or finding evidence to support generalizations. Because of its open-ended nature in terms of definition, time, and application, this and the following types of learning are more difficult to attain in classroom and distributed settings.

Synthesis: Creatively applying prior knowledge and skills to produce a new or original whole. This level of learning requires combining higher-order cognitive abilities such as flexibility and long-term memory. It is also the product of continued time and effort commitment, including large amounts of practice and experience in varying situations.

Evaluation: Judging the value of material based on personal values/opinions, resulting in an end product, with a given purpose, without real right or wrong answers. To reach this level of expertise requires a high level of curiosity about the subject matter in order to endure long-term mental commitment and practice and produce novel insights.

Once you have a clear idea of your target expertise level, you can focus on maximizing effect and economy by applying appropriate instructional techniques and delivery media. The following figure summarizes the match-ups.

Increasing Expertise → (Novice / Procedural knowledge → Expert / Declarative knowledge)

	Knowledge	Comprehension	Application	Analysis	Synthesis	Evaluation
Education Sophistication	• Facts • Basic info.	• Facts • Concept understanding	• Use learned info. to solve discrete problems	• Using information to induce and deduce	• Combining information to create new ideas	• Creating new ideas based on beliefs and values
Instructional Techniques	Lecture Questioning Independent study	Lecture Questioning Independent study Exercises	Lecture Questioning Independent study Drill and Practice	Tutoring and small classes Tailored instruction Demonstration Experience	Mentoring Customized Guidance	Produce new ideas Demonstrate Competition
Appropriate Media	Printed materials Classroom Distributed (CBT)	Printed materials Classroom Distributed (CBT)	Printed materials Classroom Distributed (CBT)	On the job training Simulation	Dedicated study Dedicated performance High Fidelity Simulation	Cutting Edge Information Cutting Edge Tools

This admittedly oversimplified explanation brings to light several conclusions:

Conclusion #1: Most school education and corporate training only accomplishes novice level learning. It mostly includes written materials, classroom lecture, generalized computer-based instruction, and a moderate amount of exercises and drill-and-practice. There is a good reason for this; this type of training is less difficult and less costly to develop and is usable by a greater number of people. In this light, its prevalence makes sense. It should just be understood that it will not be effective for producing experts and maybe not even competence.

Conclusion #2: Greater expertise requires more individualized instruction. Instead of teaching general concepts using concrete examples, instructors must teach the higher-order thinking that goes into abstract problem solving. This is difficult to define, much less convey. This limits this type of training to circumstances where true expertise can be defined, and is recognized as a requirement, cost hurdles can be overcome. In educational settings, this may take the form of accelerated learning through tutoring and coaching extraordinary to mainstream resources. In government and industry this is usually reserved for occupations that are unusually critical or difficult.

Conclusion #3: Greater expertise requires more costly technology. While some technology makes the general population more capable, others actually serve to widen the gap between novices and experts. Technology not only creates advancements which require more study to understand, but also limits use to those who can access it. Now the process of learning a particular field entails not only learning concepts, but also how to access and use related technology and the advancements they make. This makes it more difficult for people to be generalists and leads to the levels of specialization that we see in many fields. Like individualize instruction, extremely expensive training technologies are usually reserved for critical and high-risk occupations. Taking an extreme, an astronaut or fighter pilot job entails so much risk and difficulty that it justifies the expenditure to build high-fidelity simulators (i.e., high degree of realistic display and feedback). These allow greater amounts of practice without jeopardizing human or system safety.

Conclusion #4: True expertise comes about only after long periods of dedicated study and experience with real situations or high fidelity simulation. There is just no way around this. The best way to quicken this process is to include persons who are motivated and have the necessary abilities and dedication to become experts.

We can now combine these conclusions with organizational trade-offs to make training implementation decisions.

Training Implementation

Implementing a suitable training program is no small feat. The purpose, goals, costs, and effort must be considered carefully before launching into one. Below are a set of guidelines to help frame your decision making process. The appropriateness of this advice will depend greatly on your organization's needs and resources.

The starting point for all this is to determine whether you are trying to build general competence or whether you are trying to produce expertise. For this discussion, I'm defining competence as a set of modular knowledge blocks which progress in linear fashion. It can be tested and exhibited through defined work behaviors. Expertise building, on the other hand, is characterized by somewhat detached stages of progression as a result of insight and experience. There is obviously some overlap since expert performance is synonymous with a high level of competence. Although it might seem honorable to strive for expertise, this might not always be practical or even desirable.

The main organizational trade-offs to consider in your decision are:

- Numbers of trainees
- Job/task characteristics
- Ease of defining performance and enabling factors
- Cost
- Physical location of trainees
- Available technology

So, let's start with competence building and move to expertise. We'll then look at some alternatives for creating competence and expertise outside of a formal training program.

Competence Building

As discussed, the majority of educational and corporate training is aimed at the lower end of Bloom's taxonomy. This provides concept introduction to large numbers of people in order to build a framework of understanding that can be later combined with experience. If this is indeed your goal, then classroom training and simple printed and electronic media are cost-effective ways to accomplish it. In addition, directed or self-study has been made easier through public on-line resources. In fact, greater access to on-line resources has greatly reduced the amount of training needed for learning common software applications. Do not, however, confuse concept and procedural learning with expertise.

One cost-efficient technique to create greater levels of declarative knowledge is to record successful demonstrations of expert performance in a video/audio documentary format. The strategy here is not so much to teach the trainee about a specific concept, but rather to create examples that illustrate deeper levels of analytical and creative reasoning. The idea is to create insight.

Insights like this help take the trainee to new plateaus in expertise. By capturing the instruction on this type of media, you maintain the cost efficiency advantage of mass presentation.

Making a further reach toward expertise requires combining instruction with experiences. A more resource intensive, but more collaborative and potentially effective technique is to create a simulated training environment where the trainee(s) must solve realistic problems at an accelerated pace. In this setting, the trainee is presented with one or more problem sets and has easy access to fellow experts, information, and feedback. Although a contrived situation (in the sense that the real world doesn't work this way), the direct contact with experts and immediacy of feedback communication create an effective and efficient way to develop hands-on experience that can lead to heightened expertise. It is a form of drill-and-practice in a somewhat realistic setting. The difficult trick here is to create situations that use realistic processes and information and that are meaningful enough to motivate the trainee to perform well.

The extent to which individual instruction and technology is used in competency and expertise building initiatives will depend on a host of factors, and is too company specific to provide prescriptive advice. Of course we would like to provide one-on-one tutoring and mentoring, as well as advanced tools to each employee. But except for extreme instances, this isn't feasible. As a general rule of thumb, when the number of trainees is greater or distributed, electronic instruction may be more cost effective. In sharp contrast to a few decades ago, modern web-based technologies have lowered the technology cost barrier to the point where it is always worth considering on a cost basis when conveying simple and interactive instruction. More costly techniques, such as simulation should be studied on a case-by-case basis, as discussed below. Human administered techniques are less costly and more effective when the number of trainees is small and when one-on-one instruction and demonstration is important.

One specific recommendation I can make is to treat instructional development as a project, and follow a structured model. In the fast pace of business there can be the tendency to assign instructional development to technical savvy individuals who can craft interesting visual presentations. While the instruction might be interesting, it may not be effective. Instructional Systems Design (ISD) is a widely accepted approach for developing effective instruction. There are many models that fall under the ISD umbrella, but most are based on or show some resemblance to the ADDIE model. The letters in the acronym represent the first letters of the model's five phases:

- Analyze – tasks and actors are analyzed to determine training needs and conditions
- Design – learning objectives and strategies are defined
- Develop - training materials are developed in a structured fashion
- Implement – training is conducted according to the design strategies
- Evaluate – the effect of training is assessed using criteria defined in the analysis phase

By following an engineering approach such as this you will have better coordination among the various people providing input. You will also have a better chance at producing instruction that addresses learning needs.

Expertise Building

As discussed, mastery is not achieved through simple knowledge acquisition or incidental experience, but rather through large amounts of concentrated practice or problem-solving, applying skills to various contexts, and gaining insights from other experts. It provides the ability to see both the big picture as well as drill down into the abstract details needed to solve specific problems. Historically, people learned skilled trades as apprentices, working along side experts in real work settings. They observed expert behaviors and were given responsibility for a certain amount of productivity. This strategy, also referred to as on-the-job training, is actually very appropriate for building expertise, but seems largely lost in today's workforce due to the pressures of competitiveness. Instead, there is more reliance on canned training, independent certification, and self-guidance. Productivity in many settings is both difficult to measure and monitor, and in some cases it may not even be important (i.e., true experts are not always needed).

High levels of expertise are typically required in jobs that are:
- High risk or critical (firefighting, physicians),
- Difficult (performers, surgeons),
- Specialized (scientists, priests),
- Competitive (business ownership, athletics)
- Collaborative (command and control centers).

It is these types of jobs that you should consider the more time consuming and costly alternatives of mentoring, simulation, and competition.

Ironically, the easiest step toward expertise building is to simply promote employee engagement in order to create on-the-job experience. One striking thing I've observed over and over is the lack of anticipation by organizations when it comes to orienting new employees. I've witnessed managers not knowing that new hires were beginning work assignments, new employees not having office space or desks, and the approach to take it easy on new employees by having them take a multitude of generalized training courses or withholding assignments until they "get comfortable". In actuality, this is more likely to promote feelings of anxiety or poor work habits. From our understanding of human abilities, preferences, and motivation, organizations should in fact take the opposite tact. As an organizational strategy, they should prepare new employees with the tools they need to do their jobs and saturate their time with challenging assignments and ready assistance to set the desired work tempo and quickly build expertise and confidence. We can all probably remember projects that were particularly difficult and intense and that required us to stretch beyond our mental resources. Although trial-by-fire may have been unpleasant, and in all likelihood you may have experienced failure, you probably walked away learning a great deal. This may sound harsh, but by following these guidelines and mixing in incentives and teambuilding functions, you can create an environment that is productive and motivating. And don't forget, people do come to work to perform work.

In some settings it makes sense to commit an investment into simulation techniques. What usually comes to mind when we think of simulation are the high tech simulators associated with airliner and spaceflight cockpits. These high fidelity simulators replicate important sensory, perceptual, and informational aspects of these critical and risky jobs. And despite their high cost, using them for training is actually more cost effective (and safe) than using the real systems.

There are several trade-offs to consider when making a decision to implement simulation:

- What volume of trainees can we expect?
- What will be the average cost per trainee?
- What is the cost of simulation vs. the cost of real system operation?
- And most importantly, what are you true <u>needs</u>?

Regarding the last consideration, despite the attractiveness of high fidelity simulators, simulation can take simpler, less costly forms. In many cases, it is not critical to simulate all aspects of a job or task. By examining sub-tasks and determining what aspects are important or difficult, you may be served well by part-task simulation. As mentioned, the cost of visual-oriented simulation has dropped substantially with the cost of software and monitors. This makes it a worthwhile technique for high volume training, such as for student drivers. In this case, fidelity is high for some aspects such as using the visual field to survey intersections and other vehicles, but lower for others such as understanding how a car will behave when losing traction. Thus, it is important to recognize precisely what is being addressed by the simulation and decide whether other techniques are needed to supplement training. Recognize too that some aspects are easier to simulate than others. For instance, there are a multitude of athletic training devices (e.g., rowing machine), which are a form of simulation. Athletes use them with success to simulate the muscular-skeletal movements that they will use during competition. The mental preparation and execution exhibited during competition is much more difficult to simulate. Some machines attempt to emulate competitive settings by adding in an electronic opponent, but the true competitive setting is difficult to replicate. The need to generate realistic examples and conditions is a common challenge for both classroom and simulated settings. The mistake often made is to believe that increasing sensation and perceptual fidelity will solve this problem, but the problem is more of an issue of "meaningfulness". We will see this same issue arise in relation to usability testing.

In summary, it is important that simulation doesn't get implemented based on a coolness factor. It needs to reflect important aspects of the task and implement proven training techniques such as performance feedback measures and guidance. To increase efficiency, identify smaller scope part-tasks that can be trained to increase automaticity and then performed within the larger task later. Consider part tasks that are performed frequently, or that are especially critical or difficult.
When feasible, supplement hands-on training with documented cases of expert performance.

Organizational Knowledge Sharing

Another approach organizations take in an attempt to accelerate the expertise acquisition process is to transfer expertise from senior to entry personnel. One problem most every organization struggles with is how to capture the intellectual capital of their experts in order to "keep it from walking out the door." Various techniques under the umbrellas of knowledge management and training have been attempted. One strategy is to elicit knowledge and maintain a knowledge base of this along with other organizational information. These efforts are conducted with good intention, but success is rare. The primary limitation stems from the nature of expertise; it is difficult to express. Documenting it requires structure and conveying it in a way that it takes a minimal amount of effort to read and interpret. This can be done successfully with concepts, facts, and rules, but is more difficult with the knowledge used to troubleshoot, make intuitive decisions, and test hypotheses. And even when it can be articulated, students will be slow to internalize it until they utilize it in some experiential setting.

Related to this is the trade-off between generalizability and specificity. If the expert documents examples that are specific, it may not interest someone solving a different type of problem. If they over generalize, then they risk leaving out enough detail needed to address the problems at hand. In the end, the system will only be as good as the information that goes into it. Maintenance is another significant hurdle. Folder and file systems are awkward for keeping information parsed and up-to-date. Newer systems using linking techniques hold more promise for search and retrieval, but still have maintenance issues.

Thus, knowledge sharing efforts are most likely to be successful in situations with well defined scopes and goals, where information can be applied without large amounts of review and interpretation. This is most often found in jobs and tasks that are rule-based and procedural. Note that these are the same types of situations that can be addressed by classroom and other types of low cost training. These jobs require some level of competence pertaining to knowledge and procedures, but not necessarily expertise. So in essence, this should be considered as another technique to be compared and contrasted within that family of alternatives.

Another strategy organizations have attempted to use to develop expertise is to promote knowledge sharing through the use of collaboration and educational tools. Recently, there has been a proliferation of collaboration tools aimed at providing the capability to chat in secluded forums, share documents, view presentations in real time, present data in immersive environments, etc. Unfortunately, these like other technologies are often acquired without much insight into whether the user base actually will work in these ways. In many cases, sophisticated tools are implemented in groups that struggle with using basic email and shared folders, and go largely unused. In other cases, the group's work patterns simply don't warrant a collaborative tool, again rendering them ineffective.

Training and Expertise Recap

This chapter brought to light the important distinction between competency and mastery, or expertise and how this can be used to shape your company's training program. We now understand the different stages of learning and that particular instructional strategies are best for refresher training and competency building, while others are needed to create true expertise. Finally, we examined the issue of organizational learning and what situations are appropriate for knowledge capture efforts.

Key take-aways:
- Expertise progresses through stages – from novice to competence to mastery.
- Most education is aimed toward building competency.
- Reaching mastery is resource intensive, requiring concentrated practice and experience.
- Organizational sharing tools are best suited for tasks where scope and goals are well defined.

Puzzle Piece 3: Technology Insertion and Interface Design

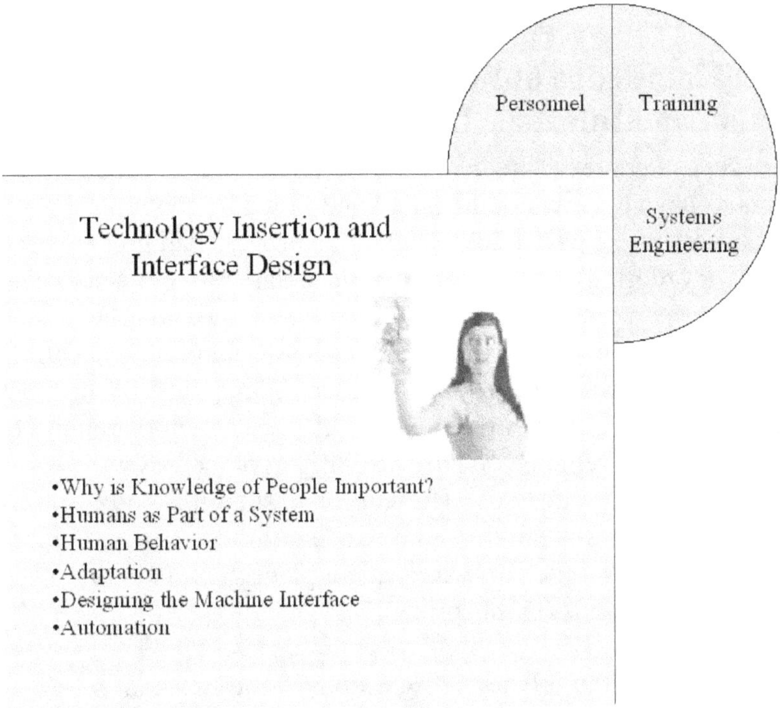

As a program or project manager or developer, you may be searching for solutions to the following technology insertion and design questions:

- What do the end users of this product really want?
- How can I anticipate how users think and work?
- How should I design my product/website to address the needs of the prospective users?
- How do we create interfaces that are easy to use?
- What can we do to make people want to use the system?

* How might people use this system in unanticipated ways?
* What good and bad effects might automation have?
* How do we assess the cost/benefit tradeoff?
* What constitutes a design problem that is liable to lawsuits?

Why is Knowledge of People Important to Technology Insertion and Interface Design?

Yesterday, as I contemplated why my purchase and subsequent attempts to have a television installed had failed, I recognized several points in the past weeks where this process had gone bad: A salesman ordering only one of three necessary parts to a stand; another salesman not being able to transact a refund; and the satellite installer showing up when I was away from home because of a time error on the recreated work order. While most of the aggravation was absorbed or vented by the present actors, much of it was a result of a reliance on software-<u>driven</u> processes vs. software-<u>supported</u> processes. Humans have strengths and limits to what they know and can do. And in each of these error points it could be debated that the software system placed extra attention and expertise demands on the human.

This chapter takes the previous discussion on abilities and characteristics and adds insight into our behavior, especially when interacting with automation. As a result you will gain a better understanding as to why some systems are more usable and pleasurable than others. In addition, you will understand how to incorporate this knowledge into a workable plan in order to influence your own products and services.

Humans as Part of a System

Taking a "systems" perspective of the situation of interest, whether it be a person using software to perform a task, scuba diving, or using power tools, we can characterize the various system aspects as being part of the human, the machine, or the environment. The human is required to conform to the rules and policies of the system and use the provided tool(s) to accomplish goals. The more congruence there is between the human needs and expectations, and the design of the system/tools, the more likely the human is to perform well and form a positive opinion about the experience. Thus, system design is all about meeting human expectations and goals.

Roadways make for a good illustration of these points. It is interesting to note that the driving task is actually something that people do well, evidenced by the fact that we can do the activity for several hours without a break. It combines moderate levels of perceptual, physical, and mental requirements. However, there are challenging circumstances, and these can be addressed by studying the "system". This system in this case is comprised of a human driver/passenger(s), an automobile (machine), and the environment, which includes the roadway, signage, weather, etc. The main goals of a transportation system are to transport the person efficiently and safely. All three components can be modified to some extent. People can be restricted through licensing or improved through training, and the automobile and environment can be designed to meet human needs and offset weaknesses. The key in all three cases is understanding task requirements and how human abilities meet or fall short. Some needs were recognized early on in automotive history and we can observe evolution in vehicle design in the form of head and tail lights, windshields, and windshield wipers, which were all designed to meet human needs to see under challenging environmental conditions. Other designs, especially those involving safety are still evolving. It may seem surprising that anticipatory street signs, head rests, and center-mounted brake lights only came into widespread use within the past few decades.

The following table outlines example key human KSAO characteristics, how they translate into driving performance, and ways that performance decrements can be mitigated by modifying the driver, vehicle, or environment. Note that this is not an exhaustive list. Rather, it is intended to illustrate the high level thinking that should be done to identify the various factors that affect human systems performance. As we will see in the chapter on systems engineering, this information can be studied in greater detail to define requirements, risks, and detailed designs.

Human Characteristic	Relation to System Performance	Mitigations
Knowledge • Rules of the road • Vehicle knowledge	A lack of knowledge results in mistakes interacting with the roadway and vehicle	Modify the human through classroom and hands-on training
Skills • Psychomotor: Steering, braking, acceleration coordination	Increasing expertise reduces chance of accidents and allows attention to be allocated elsewhere.	Simulator and hands-on training can build expertise. Expertise grows with experience. Environmental consistency through the design of highways, entrance/exit ramps, signage, etc. improves predictability.
Abilities • Vision: Humans have limited ability to see in dark or glare conditions	Reduced visibility conditions lead to higher accident rates.	Vehicle design: tinted window strips, reddish dash lighting, non-glare headlamps. Environment: Black matting behind stop lights
• Attention: Humans have limits divided attention, needed to perform in complex and dynamic settings (left turns in intersections)	Accident rates are higher in complex and dynamic settings, and when distracters are present.	Environment: Reduce visual complexity at intersections. Include green arrow for left hand turns.

• Strength and range of motion	Upper limb strength and coordination are needed when turning, especially when operating large commercial vehicles.	Vehicle design: power steering and braking Environment: Adequate turn areas
Other characteristics • Behavior: People get anxious as goals become nearer (anxiety over getting through an intersection)	Heightened stress reduces attention and decision-making abilities, potentially leading to driving mistakes.	Environment: Provide anticipatory signs and lights for intersections. Include pressure plates and signal timing to reduce braking.
• Personality traits	Some personality traits such as risk taking and irritability are associated with traffic accidents and violations	Human: Screen for drivers obtaining commercial drivers licenses Vehicle design: Audio belt reminder to increase seat belt use compliance.

Human Behavior

When designing systems, behavior can be a more important consideration than knowledge, skills, and abilities. In general, it is also less predictable. People attempt to be mobile, seek out novel experiences, multi-task, pay varying amounts of attention, take risks, avoid risks, miscalculate risks, react emotionally, are clumsy, misuse tools (often creatively), steal things, justify actions such as stealing, etc. Despite the overwhelming variations of human behavior to consider, there are some generalizations that can be made. Some of these have direct implications to design, while others are useful for understanding human behavior that might or does occur when using a system.

People do not always perform activities in the same order. The key here is to design for procedural flexibility in order to prevent chronic "human error". Handwritten signs are a telltale indication of inflexible interfaces and poor design in general. An example I see frequently are signs taped onto self-service gas pumps instructing users to swipe payment cards before lifting the pump handle. This is a case where the software designers did not allow for the flexibility in the step sequence, instead assuming that all users would perform steps in one specific manner. The next time you see notes taped to a machine interface, ascertain whether it is a design band aid, intended to prevent user mistakes. Now that you are aware of this you will probably notice them more often.

People are affected by environmental situations. The greatest advantage people have over machines is their ability to consider situational variables when making action decisions. This is positively exhibited through behavior flexibility, but negatively when factors become overwhelming or stressful. Our motivation is also influenced by factors such as reward, required effort, and constraints. For instance, we tend to become more motivated (anxious) as a goal becomes nearer in time (public speaking, making a traffic light).

People are not always rational. They are guided by self-interest, emotions, defense mechanisms, etc. As described by Maslow in his hierarchy of basic needs, we focus on basic physiological and safety needs. As those become fulfilled we turn our attention to social, self-actualization, and pleasure needs. And it doesn't stop there. We adapt our expectations and have insatiable appetites for more of whatever it is we seek. We can see this played out in the larger arena of humanity's wars over resources, whether it is for land, water, riches, or power. On a personal level, we pursue happiness through our deceptive practice of acquiring the next "bauble", "geegaw", or iPhone, as discussed historically by Adam Smith, Georg Hegel, and Karl Marx.

People strive to be efficient. Regardless of whether there is true time pressure, people tend to perform tasks efficiently. This is evidenced by our reluctance to read instructions, heed warnings, restructuring work in order eliminate steps, and creating gadgets to automate tasks. Two concepts we develop to help make decision making more efficient, schemas and stereotypes, can also be important interface design tools. Schemas are sets of knowledge and processes organized in such a way that makes it easier to remember and reproduce. For instance, when you visit a restaurant you are already aware of the scenario that will take place to get seated, order food, and make payment. This is due to the fact that restaurants have adopted these similar patterns or schema. System designers should be careful to take into account familiar existing systems during the design process. Stereotypes develop from the need to base decisions on less than complete information. Because we cannot efficiently gain all possible instances of something, we develop opinions on a sample of our experiences and beliefs and make generalizations. Of course stereotype has the negative connotation of unfairness, but it also has positive implications. In the case of system design, we can use capitalize on existing stereotypes (red-hot, blue-cold; red-warning, yellow-caution; clockwise-tighten, counterclockwise-loosen, etc.) to make machine interfaces, signs, and instructions more usable. We also want to avoid violating these. For example, there are two doors at the bottom of the stairwell of the building where I work. One has a sign with the words "Emergency Exit Alarm Will Sound" in black letters. The other door, the one you are supposed to use, has a sign stating "Not an Emergency Exit" in red letters. In this case, the stereotypic association between 'use only in an emergency' and 'red' was violated, and I find myself doing a double-take each time I use these doors.

People are not always aware of why they do things. Extending the idea of efficiency, it is clear that people sometimes take action without any conscious input at all. Rather, they make ultra-quick decisions based on impressions brought about through a combination of perception and their established belief system. The phenomenon has been coined "thin slicing" (Gladwell, 2005). This again highlights the need for designers to consider stereotypes, schemas, and branding techniques as opposed to lengthy textual and auditory messages.

People are overconfident in their ability to predict probabilistic outcomes. This has been shown to be true in a multitude of studies involving investing, gaming, and problem solving in the workforce. The common conclusion is that people form hypotheses and focus on future additional information that supports them. The result is that they take into account fewer alternative outcomes and thus underestimate risk.

People tend to focus on short-term actions instead of long-term goals. If you are in a project-oriented line of work, you can observe this in yourself and co-workers in the form of motivational peaks and valleys during project lifecycles. Although a day always equals a day, focus and motivation (stress) are lowest at the beginning of a project and greatest toward the end. When designing systems, it is important not to force the user to plan too far ahead. This can be done by breaking tasks into several intermediate steps and to allow flexibility for them to react to new information and events. Tactical tasks are easier to define, control, and predict. Longer term strategizing requires the ability and motivation to visualize and make inferences. Interceding events make outcomes less predictable, adding risk.

People are individuals, thus there will be always be variability and uncertainty about how different people will think and act. No matter how much thinking goes into system conceptualization and definition, users will find a way to surprise its designers. Users will misunderstand, misuse, and mistrust systems. It is a fact we just have to accept. This is the reason statistical analysis becomes a critical tool in the behavioral sciences. Whereas the physical world can often be defined and predicted based on laws of nature, the psychological world is probabilistic in nature, predictable only in terms of inferential statements based on assumptions and samples of evidence. This underscores the need for usability testing using representative users, which will be discussed in the systems engineering chapter.

Absent extreme life events, people carry persistent traits throughout life. Without delving into the myriad of human developmental theories or unwillingly invent my own, it is generally accepted that physical, cognitive, perceptual, moral, social, and emotional development develops rapidly in children. At some point these become more crystallized and central to one's self. We mature, and consequently our behavior and mentality matures, but basic tendencies established early in life persist. As mentioned in the chapter on personnel, this is why professionals in this arena are more and more relying on the assumption that the best predictor of future behavior is past behavior.

People's perceptions and behavior change over time, based on personal, generational, and societal factors. At first glance, this seems contradictory to the previous statement. However, what I'm suggesting is that we are beings with established identities and traits, but are constantly exposed to stimuli which cause us to reassess ourselves over time. Some aspects such as abilities are fairly resistant to change, while beliefs and social mores are more malleable. Recent evidence from studies using fMRI imaging indicates that the part of the brain that controls executive decision making does not become mature until early adulthood. This topic is so important, yet so open-ended that it is difficult to know how to begin applying it to product design. The following discussion on adaptation, however, provides an approach for understanding, influencing, and monitoring the impact of personal change.

Adaptation

Deservedly, there is much excitement over recent advancements in neuroscience. fMRI, EEG, and other brain activity measurement techniques have brought new understanding of the way our brains process information and create action. We can accurately identify the regions of the brain that are responsible for doing particular functions. We can even determine patterns that different individuals rely on and that result in varying levels of ability. For instance, Kozhevnikov, et al. (2005) make a convincing argument that individuals differ as to the neural pathways they use when performing visual tasks, and this greatly explains why they are better at some tasks versus others (e.g., visualizing folded surfaces versus seeing objects in degraded visual scenes). I am a little concerned by books and people that read them making bold proclamations about people in new generations possessing brains that "are wired differently". While I do believe in individual and generational differences, I think it is safe to say that human information processing has remained constant – we all still tend to form synaptic networks and regions in the same way as our ancestors. And this results in the same set of human emotions and behaviors. What I do believe accounts for generational differences is cultural adaptation, resulting from an increase in the amount and speed of information and stresses from society as a function of population growth.

Adaptation Theory

In 1953[2], Harry Helson postulated the Theory of Adaptation Level which attempted to explain how people make perceptual judgments about the physical world (e.g., the brightness of light, heaviness of weight) as well as cognitive and social phenomenon (e.g., reactions

---

[2] I possess a seminal 1953 article written by Helson titled "The Theory of Adaptation", whose whole reference is unknown. It appears to be a product resulting from a government contract. I have mentioned the correct historical year, but referenced the publically obtainable 1964 book.

to stress, darkness of skin color). Although original in title, his theory is undoubtedly influenced by Charles Darwin and other early developmental theorists. Helson noted that people have the tendency to respond in varying degrees of acceptance or rejection to objects, people, or statements (i.e., good - bad, beautiful - ugly, desirable – undesirable). Somewhere in between is a neutral position which the person considers the stimuli to be centered or "normal". The positioning of the center can be established either by a real stimulus that is referenced due to its intensity, novelty, frequency, emotional connotation, value or some other reason, or by some imaginary mental standard. Experimental evidence suggests that this center can move over time and be influenced by new experiences, residuals from past experience, and the context surrounding experiences. The extent to which experiences change the position of the central reference point depend on recency, frequency, intensity, nearness, and emotional factors.

In our case, this theory provides a good way of understanding how a person's expectations change. One's standard of living makes for a good case. At a macro-level perspective, economic and generation related conditions can have great influence over our perceptions. A robust economy and technological advances raise the bar, both on a personal and organizational level. As wealth is generated people purchase experience new foods, products, and services that become the new norm (clean water, meat, electronics, automobiles, vacations). This new norm will persist until further influences change the reference point.

In the United States, the 10-year period between 1925 and 1935 illustrated how quickly the reference point of an entire society can change. A period of prosperity led to an escalation of standard of living expectations during the 1920s. More and more people created artificial wealth by increasing amounts of leverage in the stock market (margin ratios of 20:1 were allowed as compared to 2:1 in today's market). When the market crash of 1929 occurred, the focus was no longer on luxuries, but on necessities. The distinction between needs and wants again became obvious. Similar, albeit less detrimental stock market bubbles were experienced in Japan and within the technology sector in the United States during the course of the 1980s and 90s. Polled investors routinely stated that they expected year over year returns on the average of 20 –25% in the stock market, despite a widely recognized fact that historically the average return was around 10%. Again, when the markets returned to earth noticeable changes in consumer and investment behavior ensued. Once the recency of these corrections faded, consumers again succumbed to their desire for higher living, leading to a bubble in the housing market. In 2008 and beyond, we again witnessed a readjustment of reality when the housing bubble burst.

We too can observe the standard of living bar being raised over generations. Technological advancements combined with easier credit and a "spend now – pay later" societal attitude cause ever-quickening adaptation to new ideas and products. This is evidenced by statistics related to market growth of several mainstream products over recent generations. Whereas it took 38 years for radio to reach 50 million users, it took just 13 years for television and 5 for the internet. The International Telecommunication Union suggests that the number of worldwide mobile cellular subscribers reached 50 percent in early 2008. Today, children who do not own their own computer with internet access are considered disadvantaged in the classroom.

A person's experience and maturation also influence their standard of living expectations. As children, our parents provide for our needs and wants, thereby greatly influencing what we initially view as neutral. As we become acquainted with expendable income and credit we gain experience with new products and services. Some of these will lead to changes in our expectations. This, along with the trend of increasing income over adulthood, explains why persons more often increase the standard of products and services they use. Reductions typically result from specific event drivers, such as a loss of income, while additions often have less of a rational basis.

Reflecting on the specifics within the Theory of Adaptation, those experiences that are most intense, novel, frequent, valuable, or emotion provoking will help to set the neutral point. People will tend to value different things that money can buy; some will value cars, some homes, some vacations, some freedom. These ideals will frequently be adopted from ideals of significant persons in their lives early on, and modified as they gain new experiences. Our ideals, especially related to money and material possessions, are often emotionally loaded due to positive or negative experiences we had during impressionable years. Thus, someone who has lived in poverty has likely made some strong associations to their emotional experiences at the time. Oddly, the consequential behaviors and values that result are not always consistent. Some develop miserly tendencies even as conditions improve, while others may become frivolous and never learn to respect money. Still others may identify the experience as a transient period and develop healthy attitudes toward money.

The quality and subsequent expense of items they value will also be set and adapt. Thus, people living in affluent areas who see neighbors driving expensive automobiles come to see that as the norm and are more apt to feel entitled to one as compared to those from less affluent locations. One person may not have experienced or known anyone who has used a computer, and therefore does not value one, while another not only sees them as a necessity, but insists on spending a disproportionate amount of income on state-of-the-art equipment.

My point is that we are experiencing generational adaptation with respect to computers, speed of events, etc. In his 1970 (back when life was simple!) book Future Shock, Alvin Toffler speaks of the "...uncontrolled acceleration of scientific, technological, and social change subverting the power of the individual to make sensible, competent decisions." While we indeed see signs of this, we also see both voluntary and involuntary adaptation. At work and home, we have raised the bar on "productivity" through the use of new technologies and greater expectancies. We use computers and other technologies so routinely that it is hard to imagine not having them (think of selling a house without a fax machine or computer). Oddly enough, many technologies are created with the intention of easing the "human burden", while instead the saved time is simply spent on other activities. The new pace simply becomes the norm.

We have also come to realize that children are capable of learning both mental and physical skills at a younger age and have immersed them in highly structured and demanding training programs in an attempt to have them realize their full potential. Being young and hungry for stimulation, they have come to expect constant structured activity, and when not provided with it, explored "alternative" activities on their own at alarmingly earlier ages. Easier access to information, people, and money further enable this. A product of this trend is an increasing amount of competition and specialization. In an attempt to produce the next prodigy or at least keep their kids from "falling behind" parents are enrolling kids at younger ages into concentrated studies and activities. Realizing that competition is no longer on a local scale, kids are becoming specialized in an attempt to compete on a more global level. This acts to raise the normative standard of success, while limiting the variety of experiences children partake.

This theory can be a powerful basis for the military to understand the thought processes and behaviors of foreign cultures and leaders, especially when it comes to change. Using recognized psychological and social models, we can create profiles of a person or culture that provide insight into how they are likely to behave or make decisions in given situations. Change, according to adaptation theory, occurs through new experiences, modified by residuals from past experience and the context surrounding these experiences. Change in perspectives and behavior are more likely to occur when experiences are recent, frequent, intense, near, and carry emotional impact. An interesting phenomenon related to the on-going conflict in the Middle East has been various groups' reactions to Al-Qaeda. In many instances local tribes have stood up to fight against them. But it isn't always the U.S. actions that have led to this. Rather, the people rebelled against the suicide bombings that result in random deaths among non-military targets. These incidents certainly qualify as intense, near, and emotional. The shock to the current belief system results in rapid change.

Adaptation in Business

Regarding business systems and the people who use them, we must understand the changes that are taking place and design accordingly. Workers and households must process increasing amounts of information and tools, especially that which is computer-based. Instantaneous collaboration with people and web-based information provides the basis for efficient learning and fact gathering. Because of tool accessibility, better product quality and speed is expected. People are assumed to possess a greater baseline of skills, or at least be capable of self-training. Despite the pressures that these advances bring, it has been noted that intelligence levels have been in an uptrend over the past few decades. As mentioned above, kids are being exposed to educational information at earlier stages. As an example, I have noticed that children appear to be more capable of multi-dimensional thinking. One observation is that my children's simple computer game has them selecting players to a team based on different athletic skill dimensions. In talking to them, it is apparent that they realize the idea of quantifiable strengths and weaknesses and how it will affect the game. I don't believe that the ability to reason in this way was as prevalent among young children a generation ago.

I have expounded a great deal on adaptation theory for the reason that it is a big driver for human thinking and behavior. And it is not only part of a person's make-up, but also something that you as a business person can influence. Let's take the idea that recency and emotional effects influence the adaptation of one's perceptions, and apply that to an example of customer satisfaction.

The problem with customer satisfaction, and subsequent loyalty, is that they are based to a great extent on perception and can be totally determined (good or bad) by a single experience. Having web application experience, I'm admittedly hyper-vigilant about poor designs when I have to use them. I once attempted to book an airline ticket using Northwest Airline's website. After researching all options and proceeding through the payment process, I received a "No existing account" message. Knowing that I had an account, I attempted to recreate it and other variations, at which each time I was informed that the account already existed. After cycling through this inescapable loop several times, I assumed there was a software glitch and gave up for the night. As can be predicted, the flight cost $150 more eight hours later. A plea to the phone assisted agent did not help. At that point I booked my flight with another airline and always had that incident in the back of my mind. It gets worse than that. Now every time I interface with that airline I am sensitive to any new negative experience, and it seems that something occurs every time. Whereas I might shrug off grounded planes, impersonal service, and poor communication as part of the industry as a whole, I always seem to have an acute memory (perception) of the accumulation of incidents with Northwest.

This can work the other way, too. A unique and satisfying experience can hook a customer instantly, and as long as future experiences are consistent, that customer can be the best marketing tool you'll ever have. When I purchased my last car, I visited two dealerships on the same day. The first pulled all the classic 30-year outdated sales techniques: new salesman with no information or sales closure power, bait and switch, fuzzy numbers, delay then time pressure, bad mouth trade-in and competitor cars, selling used as new, etc. After an hour I decided not to buy anything from this dealer. After another hour of being way too polite, I drove off in my own car, which was looking a lot better now.

Thirty minutes later I was being given good advice about my trade-in including the opinion that I should drive it another year and come back when I was ready! Forty-five minutes after getting concise information about the car and loan, I drove the car off the lot. The experience was so refreshing, I gladly refer others.

Designing the Machine Interface

Similar to the customer satisfaction experience, people will form opinions about products based on its design. So far we have seen how the people can be viewed as a multi-dimensional package of KSAOs and how that translates into the conceptual use of a system. The next step is to understand the implications this has on interface design. For this discussion, I'll keep to guidelines that pertain to the majority of users versus special cases.

In general, the steps a user takes when using a system are (Norman, 1986):
1. Establish a goal
2. Form an intention
3. Specify an action sequence
4. Execute the action
5. Perceive the system state
6. Interpret the state
7. Evaluate the system state with respect to the goals and intentions

To illustrate, let's take the case of finding the location of a restaurant using a web-based search engine. The goal is to locate the address and directions. The intention is to use a browser and search engine to locate the information. The action sequence is to type in the name of the restaurant and city, click 'Find', click on

'Map', etc. Once executed, you observe the system response in order to determine whether it provided the answers to your goals. In this fairly simple example, designers could follow standard accepted practices in order to accommodate your goals. They know that this is an activity people do frequently. They know the action sequence needs to be short and language should be simple. It is recognized that some people prefer to see the information spatially as in a map and others prefer procedural text directions, and so an optional display/print capability can be provided.

Other less frequent and more complex situations require more study to understand the best design practices. And the type of system will of course dictate whether the important characteristics are likely to be physical, perceptual, or mental in nature. Typically, software system considerations will be more demanding on perceptual and mental abilities, and more specifically vision and memory (short-term, working, and long-term). Although we may not consciously think about it, many website designs require an excessive amount of visual searching and decision making to achieve goals. Unclear terminology, excessive wording, poor organization, and unclear navigational paths combine to make many sites difficult or tiring to use. In other cases, poor interfaces between applications require excessive user actions and tax memory and attention resources.

The best example I have experienced with respect to this last point was while using the commercially available application SPSS in conjunction with Microsoft Excel. I was performing statistical work and kept a central Excel spreadsheet, which was frequently updated with information from other spreadsheets. These could be imported into SPSS, where the statistical functions were performed. I needed to generate tables and figures and include them in PowerPoint presentations. After doing this work it was apparent that although SPSS provided the capability to import data, it lacked very important capabilities that strained user's mental resources. First, although the application appeared to look like a spreadsheet, it did not perform many functions that spreadsheets provide, and thus the need to use Excel. When data was imported, SPSS reformatted the numerical formats and made incorrect assumptions about the variable attributes. I then had to use a separate attributes page to make declarations. This may have been acceptable except for the fact that updates from the spreadsheets required the entire process to be repeated. In addition, the variable attributes page was organized horizontally (headings in a column), while the main data page was oriented vertically, requiring excessive visual reorientation. Perhaps the most puzzling part came when exporting tables. They would not paste directly into PowerPoint. Instead, I had to paste them into Excel, where extra columns were added. I then had to eliminate them, resize all cells, then copy and paste into PowerPoint. Any time changes occurred, the entire sequence had to be repeated. At the end of the day, I would be mentally fatigued, as well as being more prone to make mistakes. This was either a case of designers not looking beyond the simple use case where someone used the data solely within the application, or a case where they didn't care enough to fix it.

Related to the previous example is the premise of a book on website design, Don't Make Me Think (Krug, 2000). The author makes the argument that any time a question mark pops into someone's "thought balloon" while using a website represents a situation where workload is added and the potential for interface improvement exists. And while some design issues are more important than others, all contribute to the ultimate usability of the site. The same argument holds true for other types of systems as well.

So, how do we go about determining the important human characteristics to consider when designing a system? To reach a precise answer, a job or task analysis may be necessary to capture details. At an exploratory level, the following thought process can give you a general sense:
- Who are the users?

- Are tasks physical, perceptual, or mental in nature?
- Characterize the relevant abilities further by using the taxonomy in the Personnel Selection chapter.
- Which KSAOs will be required most frequently?
- Which KSAOs will be required during the most critical tasks?
- Which KSAOs will be required during the most difficult tasks?
- Are age differences in vision, hearing, mental ability, mobility, strength, etc. likely to influence performance?
- Do any extreme characteristics such as height and weight need to be considered?

Delving into these questions allows you to focus on design principles that promote successful and safe systems use. In the case of extreme task demands or user characteristics, you can develop designs based on extraordinary characteristics that either accommodate or aid exceptional users.

A Word on Guidelines

Many companies and independent groups have attempted to capture human factors and computer interface design guidelines in order to promote standardization. The logic is that creating usable products would simply be a matter of following established conventions. As described below, there have been some successes, although they inevitably fall short of providing developers with easy-to-follow design recipes. Guideline development efforts, as with research in general, invariably run into a generalizability vs. specificity conundrum. If the guideline is stated so that it can apply to multiple domains, it becomes too general to dictate design. On the other hand, if it is stated in the level of detail needed to dictate design, it will fail to generalize across different design situations. The middle ground where success can be attained lies in identifying situations where common design issues make the use of templates feasible (e.g., eCommerce transactions) and very specific and repeatable situations where research can dictate good design (e.g., search functions).

Indeed, using sound and familiar conventions will make the interface easier to use and reduce the number of user mistakes, and we should make an attempt to use something as a developmental north star. But simply following a set of guidelines is not enough to ensure that the product is allowing users to complete tasks efficiently and accurately. As the saying goes "the devil is in the details", and it is only through analysis, documentation, and testing that we can be confident that the design is good (or that conventions were really followed). We've all experienced situations where we could not complete web-based transactions. The next time this happens, ask yourself whether it was a matter of not following conventions or whether the site design was not compatible with your goals and actions (your goals are the details!). The following is an example where both types of error occurred. Recently, I attempted to book a room at a hotel in Las Vegas. Their website stated they were part of the Harrah's family and a link took me to the Harrah's site. Once there, there were two obstacles for completing the reservation: the specific hotel was not on the pull-down menu and the departure date field only allowed one digit. In this case, the convention of allowing two digit entries was violated, while the goal of the user coming from a related website was not supported. This is very interesting from a business standpoint. At some point, someone had to make a business case to build the website, probably on the grounds that enabling self-service on-line reservations would increase reservations and save labor cost. So it is curious as to whether they have taken notice of the volume of reservations. It has to be low, since only people leaving on dates 0-9 could use it. Secondly, no one could have _ever_ made a reservation for that specific hotel on-line. So, by virtue of these interface exceptions, not only is the self-service benefit reduced, but potential customers can easily move down the street (the strip in this case) to another hotel that has a functional website.

One of the more complete and usable set of publicly available guidelines on web site development is located at Usability.gov, and I encourage you to become familiar with the site. The authors provide guidelines organized by chapters. For each, they offer clarifying comments, research sources, one or two illustrative examples, and ratings indicating the relative importance and strength of evidence. There is also other information to help developers plan usability activities.

A couple of examples from Usability.gov help illustrate situations where guidelines are specific enough to be used easily and others where more generalized guidelines require interpretation. The first example, under the heading "Provide Feedback When Users Must Wait", is a relatively straightforward convention to implement.

Guideline: Provide users with appropriate feedback while they are waiting.

Comments: If processing will take less than 10 seconds, use an hourglass to indicate status. If processing will take up to sixty seconds or longer, use a process indicator that shows progress toward completion. If computer processing will take over one minute, indicate this to the user and provide an auditory signal when the processing is complete.

The second example, under the heading "Reduce the User's Workload", is more generalized, and even with the provided examples requires interpretation to determine how to implement it. In other words, to implement this guideline, you need to know the user goals and task sequences they are performing.

Guideline: Allocate functions to take advantage of the inherent respective strengths of computers and users.

Comments: Users learn certain sequences of behaviors and perform best when they can be reliably repeated. For example, users become accustomed to looking in either the left or right panels for additional information. Also, users become familiar with the steps in a search or checkout process.

In my experience, I have found guidelines to be helpful in the sense that they provide structure about how to think about an interface. By reflecting on them, you can combine previous knowledge and opinion as to whether the interface accomplishes their spirit. You can develop your own example library to help illustrate and construct implementations. You can also construct checklists and use them to report usability judgments and status, as will be described shortly. The more theoretical and practical experience you have using guidelines, the better you will be able to use them as "thinking" tools.

Metrics

You may be tempted or forced at some point to quantify the usability of an interface. Quantification seems to give people comfort and confidence that go beyond non-quantitative opinions. Even when the validity of measures and scaling are questionable, numbers can be quite convincing. There certainly are cases where quantification is useful when done properly.

One potential use of metrics is to summarize the results of user performance during usability testing (described in the next chapter). The time needed to perform tasks, numbers of errors, questions, etc. can be measured in order to assess performance associated with design changes. One pitfall to be mindful of when measuring performance is creating conflicting conditions between the data you are capturing and the test environment. This usually occurs when testers try to capture both time and error data, but encourage participants to explore and vocalize. It is easy to see why this is desirable; testers want participants to act naturally and they want to understand what they are thinking. But at the same time, a) this is not how people naturally perform, and b) the time data is affected by the participant talking and exploring. Time confounding becomes even more pronounced when repeated trials are performed, since participants tend to vocalize and explore more on the first trial and be more procedurally efficient on subsequent trials. On the other hand, if participants are encouraged to perform optimally and not vocalize, their opinions will change by the time they finish or repeat the task. You get a lot of responses like "I didn't understand it at first, but now that I've done it I could do it easily." Because one approach usually compromises the other, a good strategy is to split participants into the two instruction camps and treat them as separate usability tests.

A second use for usability metrics arises when needing to make comparisons between products. One effective and cost-efficient technique I recommend is to create a user-centered evaluation framework based on sound usability principles. This framework should consist of 50-80 ratings and address accepted usability guidelines that can be found in the general literature (such as usability.gov) or created by a usability practitioner. These should be as specific as possible. For example:

- Procedural sequences contain a minimal number of steps
- Users can easily recover from recent steps (Back and Undo functions)
- Links are ordered and grouped logically
- Terms are understandable to the novice user (no technical jargon or undefined acronyms)
- The status of the current procedure is explicitly stated

You can then use this framework as a scorecard to evaluate the interface(s). Begin by identifying a set of tasks that users will be performing. Have 2-3 evaluators exercise the application and discuss incidents where the interface meets or fails to meet each guideline. Discuss the importance of each guideline and create a scoring system to summarize the ratings. Ratings can be grouped by themes in order to consolidate them for reporting purposes. By using multiple and interacting raters you will uncover more incidents as well as improve ratings stability. Although these ratings are still based on subjective opinions, they do provide a systematic way to assess the usability of an interface. Note that since these guidelines represent good interface qualities, they can be equally effective for use during the interface development phase.

The subject of good and poor interfaces makes this a good point to discuss automation, the reason why these interfaces are being designed in the first place.

Automation

As long as humans have been making tools they have consciously or unconsciously made decisions about what aspects of a task to delegate. Shovels provide sharp edges for digging that human hands lack; abacuses lessen the load on short-term and working memory; telescopes allow us to detect light beyond the capability of our natural eyesight. Computers and electronics have opened the floodgates to automated systems to the point where human and system interaction is ubiquitous. It is important for system developers to recognize the proper opportunities to implement automation, and as such important to understand why humans are using it and what about them affects how and how much automation will be used.

Automation is introduced into systems for three main reasons:
1. To relieve people from tasks that they do not want to do. This may be due to a task being dangerous (defusing bombs, painting automobiles), undesirable (monitoring gauges, cleaning floors), or because they wish to do other tasks. If you know a realtor who has been in the business a long time, ask them if they can imagine going back to the days before fax machines, where they were required to personally deliver each offer and counter-offer between buyer and seller.

2. To improve accuracy and efficiency. Machines and humans are better at doing different things. Machines are better at calculating numbers, monitoring, withstanding hostile environments, and making rule-based decisions. Humans are better at adapting to different circumstances and making decisions based on uncertain information and intuition.
3. To save money through reduced human labor. We can witness this trend across time in almost every industry. A few easily recognized examples include telephone switchboard operators, factory assembly line tasks, and weapon system cockpits.

Interestingly, despite wishful thinking, automation does not result in people working less hours at the office and consequently having more free time. Instead, studies show that the time saved is used to complete additional work, resulting in increased productivity.

The success of automation lies in the extent to which users accept and properly use it. As a system designer or acquirer, you should take the following variables into account when introducing automation:

- Benefits. Benefits can come in the form of time, cost, convenience, etc. This seems to be an obvious result of automation, but in practice can be more difficult to express. Because of uncertainties about development, the population of users, amount of use, comparison system costs, and competitive systems it is sometimes difficult to predict what future benefits will be.

- Amount of control. This relates to the extent to which actions are allocated between machine and user. This ranges from simple tools where humans have complete control over operation and subsequent actions (a calculator) to a system where computers have complete autonomy and are self-regulated. Most system automation lies somewhere in the middle and can be more accurately labeled semi-automation. In this mode, machines have been designed to accomplish sub-tasks, while a human user maintains control over goal setting and other sub-tasks.

- Trust. This refers to the extent that a user deems a system to be accurate and reliable, and has a direct effect on system acceptance and use rate. Recent experimental work (Merritt & Ilgen, 2008) suggests that a person's trust in automation is a dynamic relationship. Users have an inherent disposition towards automation, and this greatly influences their willingness to initially use the system. Trust then evolves over time as the user gains experience and judges its usefulness and dependability. Interestingly, extroverted individuals tend to have greater initial trust, but then react more negatively to poorly performing systems than do introverts.

It is important to note that there is an optimal level of trust that lies somewhere between blind faith and total mistrust. In other words, systems can be both under and over trusted, and the best combination is letting machines do what they do best and letting humans monitor and override actions when necessary. I recently experienced first-hand a case of system over trust with respect to my real estate tax assessment. After seeing my neighborhoods' assessments rise 23% in a year where the county average stayed equal, I explored the calculations. Upon inspecting the comparison properties it became clear that the county was relying on automation with no human "sanity check". There were zero recent valid comparison properties, so the calculations were based on land sales and other irrelevant properties. What was needed was a flag showing them where valid comparisons were lacking and statistical outliers existed so that they could manually examine extreme cases. The tax department did make an adjustment, but at the cost of time and loss of credibility.

- Use. The amount of system use depends on a combination of benefits, trust, ease of use, and the extent to which they are required to use it. This is situation specific and changes over time.

- Misuse. This reflects ways that people use products in a way that was not intended by the manufacturer. This is an important issue for manufacturers, as misuse exposes them to costly litigation. Mitigations usually involve labeling and designing products to prevent misuse. One example that illustrates the struggle of warning designers is the fact that a significant number of people die each year when heating their homes using charcoal grills.

An example that illustrates these factors is the widely used tax preparation software applications, such as Turbo Tax. The complexity of the United States tax code has rendered completing tax returns using paper forms ineffective for the majority of citizens claiming itemized deductions. Not only does it require high levels of concentration and decision making, inevitable modifications make the task unduly, time-consuming, and prone to error. I personally gave up on paper returns when capital gains were broken up into long and short-term, turning Schedule D (Capital gains) into spaghetti logic. Two options are to give the job to a tax preparation specialist or purchase a semi-automated application to replace the manual task. The costs and benefits are fairly clear. For $20-$50, you are guided through a set of interview questions which then map the answers onto the appropriate forms and schedules. You have control over the numbers you enter, the pace and mode of entry (forms vs. interview), and can override the system when necessary. There are also issues of trust and misuse. The relative ease of entry and neat appearance of the final product may give the user a false level of confidence that the return is correct. The fact of the matter, however, is that these applications are not much more than spreadsheets with a modified data entry strategy. Errors arise by way of misinterpretation of tax rules by programmers and misinterpretation of questions by the user. Various tax preparation software applications have been shown to provide inconsistent results in head-to-head comparisons. On the other hand, obvious errors lead to lower confidence, mistrust, and user acceptance. This enforces the design principal of visibility. Systems should make their reasoning transparent so that the human can override decisions as necessary. With respect to Turbo Tax, I have had it declare that I need to file estimated quarterly taxes when it was clearly not the case. Without a window to their logic, it is unclear how the application made that decision, lowering my trust. My intuition is that people may be more inclined to misuse applications to cheat. My hypothesis is that the neat appearance combined with a separation of responsibility introduced by automation ("the computer is doing it and therefore shares responsibility") could lead to inadvertent and not so inadvertent mistakes.

Of course, one of the main business goals in a capitalistic society is to be more cost effective than the competition. This has been a major reason for the push to replace most business' greatest cost, human labor, with automation. As you will see below, replacing people with machines involves a host of other considerations.

A Comparison of Systems

Let's consider three examples of systems that have introduced automation for the purpose of replacing human labor with machines: automated teller machines (ATMs), self-serve gasoline stations, and self-serve retail check-out machines. They were all implemented with a common purpose; that is to save the business owner money. Simplistically, the return on investment is the savings in human labor minus the cost of purchasing and maintaining the machine. And, based on economics, the decision to implement these systems is probably an easy one. But, taking a systems view, we can see how each of these systems changes the rules and relationships between the business and customer. In each case, how do these systems change the customer experience? How does it change workload allocation? Are there benefits to the customer? How does it change the customer's perception of the business? Let's examine each one, in the order of what I consider to be customer-oriented.

The ATM, first patented in 1973, is designed to replace the human bank teller in order to save the business on labor costs. Using the machines, customers can perform a host of financial functions; most notably withdraw cash at any hour of the day. Although misuse and mistrust can occur with this system, customers can easily identify several advantages of ATMs over bank branches: they are available in widespread locations, are available round the clock, and don't require customers to enter buildings or have face-to-face contact (yes, this is sometimes very preferable). On top of that, the interfaces have become fairly standard and straightforward. Even when charges are applied, the added benefits often justify its use. In addition, the ATM has not totally replaced the physical bank, so there is always an alternative during business hours. Because both business and customer gain, I would deem this automation as symbiotic and a good use of automation.

Compare this with self-service gasoline stations, which have replaced full-service in all but Oregon and New Jersey, where by law attendants are required to pump gas. The advantage to the business are again obvious; allocating the gas-pumping and car maintenance duties to the customer allows the business to be run by a smaller and less skilled crew. And, since the customer must get out of their vehicle and enter the station if they pay in cash, they are more likely to spend money on snacks or other items. To the customer, the advantages are not as readily apparent. They must get out of their vehicles, pump their own gas, and perform any vehicle checks or maintenance themselves. This may result in less comfort and missed maintenance issues (e.g., low on oil, tire pressure). For this, they may be able to quicken the process by not having to make the transaction with an attendant. So, in this case the automation is more imposed on the customer than preferred. What is interesting here is that you don't hear people complain about it. Over time, people have become accustomed to the fact that there are few alternatives and have accepted it as they way it is.

The third example, a more recently introduced self-service retail check-out machines, throws the advantage/disadvantage balance further in the direction of the business. Like the other two, the retailer's benefit is reduced staffing requirements. Cashiers may now be able to monitor several lanes as compared to one previously. At first glance, there appears to be an advantage to the customer as well. Theoretically, the number of open lanes is not restricted by the number of available cashiers, resulting in fewer customers waiting in each line. Thus, the system is touted to increase the speed and convenience of the check-out process. In practice, however, the efficiency advantage is eroded on several fronts, most notably experience and interface issues. Customers are untrained and infrequent users of the systems. They don't move as quickly as a trained cashier. There is also a slight delay introduced after each item due to auditory feedback. Significant time delays occur when exceptions arise (e.g., such as when produce items must be researched or personal identification must be checked). The interfaces in many systems, like the one at my local grocery store, are poorly integrated with the existing payment system. Users are prompted twice to indicate whether they are using a credit or debit card. They must move backward and forward several times to complete the scanning, payment selection, signature, and receipt process. Although a repeat customer can get used to it, it is an example of poor integration, and the effect on the customer experience varies. In my opinion, this system can be beneficial for customers who are frequent users and who have a small number of "non-exception" items, but may actually be counterproductive for others.

The bigger issue may be the move away from retailers representing their customer service by face-to-face to machine interaction. I have preferred some retailers' cashiers over another, but can't say I've formed an opinion about any particular chain's self-checkout system. From a ceiling view, stores now appear as a sea of buyers fumbling through the imposed systems and procedures, with the cashiers now serving as monitors who intercede when exceptions arise (frequently). This is hardly a situation that breeds customer loyalty. After one particularly exasperating experience, I asked one of the watchwomen who was sitting on a stool at the end of my lane how the system was working out, whereby she exclaimed "We love them!" My silent reaction was that it was clear that "we" did not include "me". Unfortunately for consumers, the retail industry has bought into this trend so much that there is little choice; and most stores do offer the option of using an attended lane. But, on the bright side, so many consumers have bought into the perception that it shortens their time in line that it has shortened the queues in the cashier lines for the rest of us! It will be interesting to see how the public response to this type of system evolves with time and whether it becomes as ingrained to future generations as ATMs and self-service gasoline stations.

The Need for System "Integration"

Perhaps the best argument for system integration comes directly from real examples. Han, et al. (2006) summarized a tragic case of how the benefits of automation can go awry when system integration and measurement are performed outside of the larger context. The project centered on a commercially sold computerized physician order entry (CPOE) system, implemented in an effort to reduce medical errors and mortality among children who are transported for specialized care. By selecting drugs and seeing potential interaction warning feedback via computer screen, it was hoped that handwriting and interpretation errors would reduce mistakes. These types of errors were indeed reduced as shown by an initial study. However, anecdotal feedback from the field prompted a follow-up study that revealed that the mortality rate significantly increased from 2.80% (39 of 1394) before CPOE implementation to 6.57% (36 of 548) after CPOE implementation. The investigators attributed this to system integration and human-computer interface issues. Although orders were more accurate, they now took 1-2 minutes to enter as compared to a few seconds previously. In addition, the system required the patient to physically arrive at the facility before orders could be filled, eliminating preparatory actions that could occur under the previous procedures. These changes in dynamics proved fatal in such time-sensitive circumstances. So, although the technology holds promise as a tool to reduce human error during health care delivery, this particular implementation demonstrates the importance of integration with the larger process, including allowing for exceptions and human override.

Focusing on the User Experience

This discussion about end users, design guidelines, and automation can be summarized in the framework of a total "user experience". If the person finds their experience to be safe, beneficial, or pleasant they are more likely to approve and revisit it. One's experience includes both function and affective appeal. The majority of systems we use are there to help us carry out tasks, and thus most of this book has focused on human and machine functionality. But it is important to keep in mind that experiences can be influenced by sensual aesthetics such as colors, temperature, and sound, other person's demeanors, and many other subtleties. This is an effect that goes beyond functional satisfaction and reaches into the realm of pleasure. What do kids remember most about riding on an airplane? Answer: A soda and some peanuts (at least they used to). Some of this effect can be attributed to unconscious attributes, such as design and pricing tricks introduced by marketing professionals. Others can stem from the user's recognition that the product developer did something to recognize a user need or preference. As with functional capabilities, designers should attempt to define affective requirements. There needs to be a sensible balance to ensure that affective design doesn't actually detract from the user's tasks, as in the unfortunate case of the Microsoft Office paperclip/dog friend.

Hancock, et al. (2005), recently coined the term hedonomics to capture the idea that designers can take measures to create pleasure in human systems. Although the premise is not entirely new, they propose a greater formal recognition of systematic ways to promote it. They propose a design need hierarchy analogous to Maslow's need hierarchy. This asserts that users seek systems that are safe, functional, and useable. Once each of these successive needs is met, we then strive for experiences that are pleasurable and finally those that promote individuation; that is, systems that provide customization and flexibility to allow us to adapt.

Certainly we can see affective design play out in the restaurant industry. To varying degrees food is food, and much of a user's restaurant experience is shaped by service and environmental factors. Restaurants create themes, stimulation levels, and pricing value to appeal to targeted demographics. For niche themes, a set of expectations are set by the brand. People expect nice surroundings and quiet in high-end restaurants and relative chaos at Chuck-E-Cheese. But for middling eateries, patrons are keen to the food, service, and environment and will tend to form an opinion about the total experience that determines repeat visits and reputation. It is these situations where managers would be advantaged to understand human preferences and be flexible enough to accommodate them. So, how can a restaurant be flexible? I can see at least three ways – the trick is to seamlessly assess patron preferences and adapt. The first way is done to some extent in most restaurants – allow people to purchase varying meal proportions. The second can be accomplished by creating spaces that provide differing areas of sound and lighting level. This requires guessing or asking one's preference. The third way, which addresses one of the biggest sources of dissatisfaction, is to adapt the speed of service. There are times when patrons desire to eat quickly and others where they are making a night of it. Unfortunately, it is rare that anyone assesses that; instead, the pace of their meal is driven by the constraints of the kitchen and staff. Someone in a hurry has a poor experience when service is slow, while someone wishing a leisurely meal may be put off by highly efficient service. I would like to see someone implement a system for patrons to convey this preference, allowing them to create a customizable dining experience – and make it work in practice. I think would be an interesting and differentiating concept.

Now let's take a look at another system that provides further study into the concept of user experience. The Washington D.C. subway system claims it is in constant financial distress and that low numbers of riders is one of the problems. On the surface, this system seems to do a good job of accomplishing the two central missions of transportation systems: transport people safely and efficiently. With the exception of a few high profile mishaps involving train derailments, feet-eating escalators, and people being run over by buses, I'm sure passengers are much safer than they would be in their vehicles. Train and bus arrivals are fairly predictable, and they've even implemented signage to anticipate the arrival and direction of the next few trains. The cost and time are not trivial, but it probably represents a decent trade-off to driving for those in close proximity.

An up-close experience with the system, however, sheds some light on why the user experience may lead to low use and acceptance. The first perception one gets is that it is very difficult for a first-time user to use. When parking, the user is informed that they will need the exact amount when exiting. The only place the amount is displayed is a small sign at the entrance gate. In addition, the user must purchase a card for five dollars on which to add the parking amount. As an aside, the card became part of the process due to a highly publicized investigation that claimed employees were stealing parking fees. What was less publicized was the finding that an accounting error was the source of the missing funds. Nonetheless, the cash generating, labor-saving cards remain in place. The cards must be purchased inside the station, where again the amount required is not posted. Once inside the station, users must purchase the train fare using any one of a myriad of machines with differing interfaces that have morphed over the years due to changes in the system and payment options. Some of these machines have instructional notes written with magic marker on the interface in response to continuing confusion. When in the train and station users are presented with a multitude of indiscernible audio announcements. There is no signage within the train to help non-frequent users anticipate the next stop. Instead, they must rely on audio announcements or signs outside the train. In addition, no public restrooms and escalators that are in repair for months on end give the perception of an unfriendly system.

Perhaps the biggest issue of this system is the handling of exceptions caused by mechanical failures, documented on a regular basis in the local newspaper. As I will detail in the section on systems engineering, designing for exceptions is an often overlooked, but critical activity. In this case, users are not equipped with basic information during rail and station failures. There is no systematic way of communicating the nature of the problem, anticipated timeline, or suggested actions to users or station managers. As a result, passengers continue to arrive at closed stations and wait in line for trains that are not coming. Perhaps the best summary of this system and this chapter as a whole was stated by a local politician, "Metro workers need to stop viewing riders as robots and more like human beings."

Technology Insertion and Interface Design Recap

This chapter highlighted the need to integrate human considerations into system design in order to improve performance and to reduce costs of ownership. From highway systems to educational systems to software systems, humans need to be the central focus, since it is their performance, safety, and budget that matters. This seems to be an obvious statement, but the fact of the matter is that systems are created with ill-conceived notions of who the end users are and what accommodations are relevant.

We've examined how human characteristics and behavior are important to developers, but still need to understand how to put these insights into practice. The next chapter describes the discipline for integrating this knowledge into the systems engineering process. By doing so, we increase the chance that our systems will accommodate users and be accepted.

Key take-aways:
* Interface design needs to take into account that humans and their characteristics are part of the "system".
* We can leverage knowledge of behavioral tendencies to improve design.
* People adapt their perceptions based on internal and environmental factors.
* Users go through predictable steps when using systems, and we can use this knowledge to improve design.
* Successful automation relies on the extent to which users trust it and benefit from it.

Puzzle Piece 4: Systems Engineering

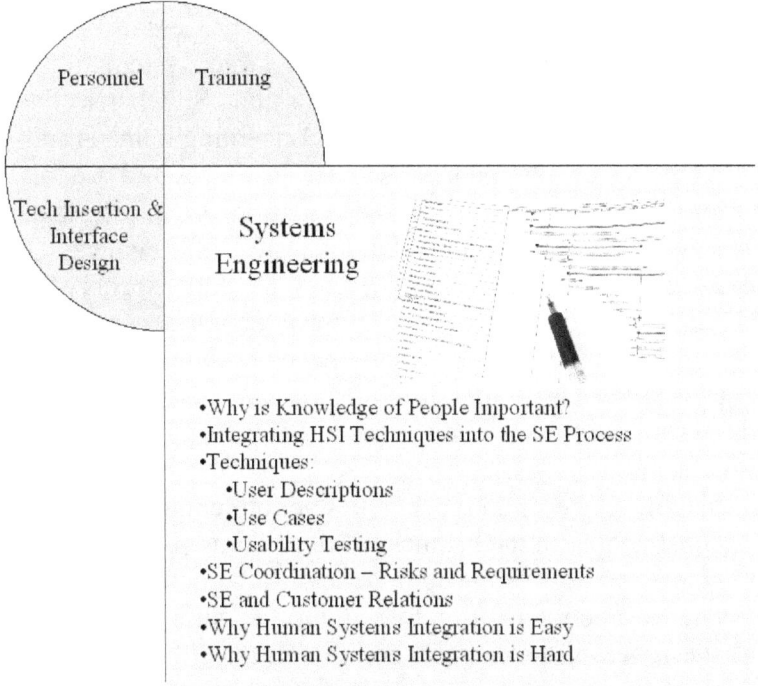

Personnel | Training

Tech Insertion & Interface Design

Systems Engineering

- Why is Knowledge of People Important?
- Integrating HSI Techniques into the SE Process
- Techniques:
  - User Descriptions
  - Use Cases
  - Usability Testing
- SE Coordination – Risks and Requirements
- SE and Customer Relations
- Why Human Systems Integration is Easy
- Why Human Systems Integration is Hard

As a project manager or systems engineer, you may be searching for solutions to the following systems engineering questions:

- ✦ What are the human-centered requirements in this project? (physical, cognitive, motivational)
- ✦ What physical risks are possible in this project?
- ✦ What acceptance risks are possible in this project?
- ✦ How can we establish better rapport with our customer?
- ✦ How can we increase usability without disrupting our development process?

Why is Knowledge of People Important to Systems Engineering?

Although the questions above are aimed largely at system design, which was covered in the previous chapter, the process of integrating human systems techniques in the larger systems engineering process deserves its own discussion. So whereas the previous chapters focused on the "what" concerning humans and product users, this chapter addresses "how" to assess and use this information during development and acquisition. One thing that has hopefully become apparent is that regardless of how fast technology and generational change occurs, the core aspects of humans remain relatively constant. The way people sense and perceive the environment, think, and behave are timeless. Knowing this allows us to look past the noise and use systematic methods to study problems in a variety of contexts.

Human systems concepts and techniques are quite understandable. As such, most people in the business of developing products have at least some awareness of the approaches. As a consequence, the human systems function is often folded into the duties of an engineer, designer, or developer who is a non-expert. The result is an implementation which may omit any formal human systems techniques. What I witness in practice is a heavy reliance on surveys and questionnaires where more powerful techniques would lead to more effective and efficient answers. While the quantitative nature of survey results is appealing for reporting purposes, the results tend to produce conclusions that are of questionable validity and do not provide insight into implementation decisions. Techniques that shift the analysis from opinion to behavioral observation provide a richer understanding of actual user behavior and performance, which in turn increases the likelihood for successfully engineering a user-centered solution. For example, I regularly provide constructive feedback to webmasters when I see problems on websites. Recently, I attempted to report a link that took me to an erroneous page. I clicked the 'Send Feedback' button. Instead of a comment box, I was presented with a survey containing four questions about whether I found the site easy to use and whether I found the information I was searching for, but no comment box. This is an example of someone seeking quantifiable data and missing the point that the user and developer really just want to fix the problem. I ended up not completing the survey because I wasn't sure how giving them a low or high score was going to help.

An additional point concerning user opinions and preferences is that they are not always correct and do not suggest the right way to design things. A good example involving power window controls comes from the website www.baddesigns.com (visit the site for thought provoking examples of poor interface design). I had a similar opinion as the web-author about the power window controls in my car. I initially found it awkward to pull back on a button in order to raise the windows. It seemed unnatural to pull up on a button, and if someone simply asked my preference, I would have stated that I want to push the button forward. However, this highlights the importance of going beyond preferences and examining potential behavioral exceptions. The pull up design makes a great deal of sense in light of incidents where children have stuck their heads out of windows while placing their hands on the controls. Requiring a lifting motion greatly reduces this accidental risk.

So, if the practice of human systems integration (HSI) goes beyond common sense, what exactly do such experts see differently than others? I'll be the first to admit that HSI experts/ practitioners aren't necessarily smarter than anyone else. Nor is it improbable that non-HSI practitioners can generate the same insights and decisions. But by their training and focus, HSI experts do tend to possess a very different perspective than other teammates. The following figure illustrates the different perspectives a developer and HSI expert bring to the team. When cultured with experience, this perspective becomes a valuable complimentary set of assets.

While the team's primary focus should remain with the developer's activities and products, the HSI practitioner provides in-depth information about the end user, allowing the team to create user-centered products and avoid usability pitfalls.

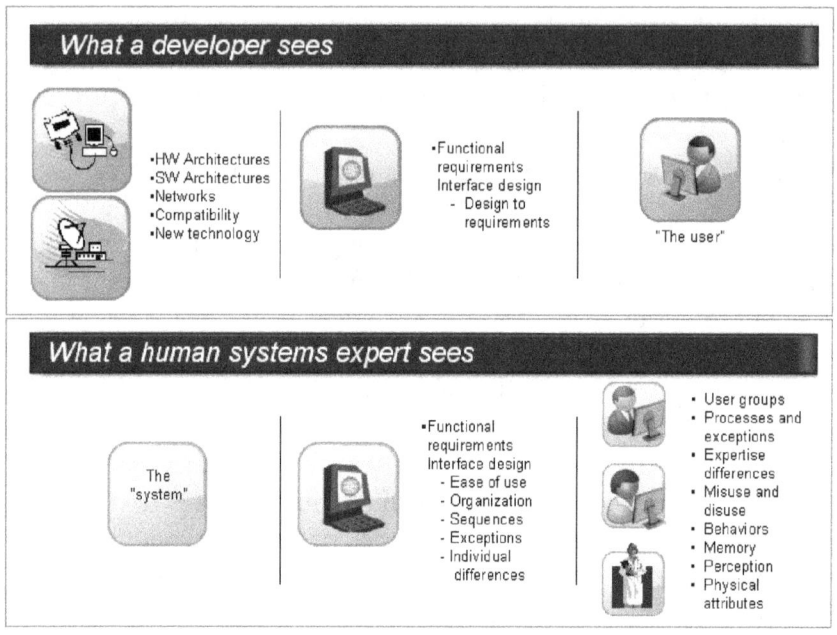

Admittedly, this figure over-generalizes the view that developers and HSI experts have little overlapping knowledge. In a given project developers will have some level of understanding of user needs and characteristics, while HSI experts will have some understanding of the technical aspects of the system. In fact, there may be instances where the HSI expert is also a technical expert and perhaps even an end user. In the appropriate settings this can provide a powerful combination of knowledge, whereby the same individual has deep knowledge of the way a user will operate in the system, and at the same time have a realistic view of the opportunities and constraints posed by technology. This dual expert combination is advantageous in systems involving user with high levels of expertise. In this situation the effort required for a naïve HSI practitioner to understand the subject matter and inner-thinking of the end user is prohibitive, and can lead to unsophisticated conclusions and frustration or indifference to the development team. Interestingly, the dual expert combination can also be a disadvantage in some projects. Such is the case when developing interfaces used by the general public. In this scenario developers can become too familiar with the system and fail to foresee potential behaviors that new users will exhibit.

Integrating HSI Techniques into the Systems Engineering Process

Aside from surveys, what else can we do to increase knowledge of user characteristics and behavior? The following sequence of figures lay out an assortment of HSI techniques and shows how they fit into the larger systems engineering (SE) process.

**Knowledge of Human Characteristics
Contributes to All Phases of the Development Lifecycle**

Development Lifecycle ➡	Phase I: Analysis	Phase 2: Design	Phase 3: Operations
SE Activities			
Human Systems Activities	Page 100	Page 101	Page 102

As you see in the figure above, the system development cycle can be divided into three phases: Analysis, Design (further broken down by Design, Development, and Test), and Operations. The subsequent figures address a single phase. In each figure, the first row details typical system engineering activities. The second row then details the human systems activities that can complement them during each phase. Again, the main objective is for these activities to add value to the larger effort. Therefore, as the project moves from analysis to development, the human systems activities begin to be less conceptual and more experiential and rigorous.

During the requirements phase techniques are used to help scope and define the project and user group. Observation and interviews, and of course surveys, can add depth to any task analyses and requirements generation that are being conducted.

Phase 1: Analysis

	Requirements Analysis
SE Activities	• Define requirements (functional, technical, performance, etc.) • Develop and choose between initial system concept alternatives • Plan system acquisition • Prepare proposal and budget

Human Systems Activities	How can HSI aid system analysis?
	• Naturalistic observation
	• Interviewing techniques
	• User-included scoping
	• Profiles
	  • Distinguish between roles and expertise
	• Task analysis
	• Use Cases
	  • Identify frequent, critical, difficult activities
	  • Identify man-machine allocation issues
	• User and organization needs definition
	• Requirements definition and traceability with use cases
	• Identify potential risks and mitigations

In the design phase human systems experts can provide guidance for interface prototypes and conduct increasingly more formal usability assessments and tests.

Phase 2: Design

	Design	Development	Test
SE Activities	• Develop and release RFP (WBS) • Contract award • Develop design concept • Develop detailed design • Develop system • Schedule management • Risk management • Requirements management • Control gate readiness • Test at factory site (FAT) • Develop and deliver initial training • Develop installation procedures • Test at operational site (SAT)		

Human Systems Activities	How can HSI aid design?
	• Develop system interface maps
	• Develop initial interface prototypes (screens or drawings)
	• Identify alternative designs and test solutions
	• Iterative usability testing (more specific with time)
	• Participate directly in developer forums (e.g., bug fixes)
	
	How can HSI aid system engineering?
	• Identify and mitigate risks
	• Manage use cases
	  - Promote use case translation to testing and training
	  - Maintain traceability with requirements
	• Participate in other SE activities (e.g., system testing, training development, on-line help, documentation based on skills)		

While it seems that human systems activities would cease after development, continuing communication with user and developer groups and post-operation usability testing can be valuable for making future improvements.

Phase 3: Operations

Operations
• Install system • User acceptance testing • Continued user training • System maintenance

How can HSI aid post-delivery acceptance?
• On-site usability testing
• User-group follow-up
• Results in next-version suggestions

How can HSI aid new release development?
• Translate new features into design
• Participate on the O&M staff to fix bugs

(Left margin labels: SE Activities; Human Systems Activities)

Two key points to reiterate are that human systems activities span the entire lifecycle and they are closely tied to other SE activities such as requirements and risk management. This affords a tremendous opportunity to the development team in that the human systems expert can not only provide information that can be reused throughout the lifecycle, but can also be the one who manages or carries out many of these activities. This provides the advantage of both information and personnel continuity as compared to efforts that lock people into positions and expect them to transfer information as the project progresses. The following figure illustrates how information created during the analysis phase flows through the requirements, design, testing, and training steps.

P.S. Could someone please invent the product portrayed in the example?

Example: Develop a Customizable TV Remote

Information from use cases provide a continuous information thread across the development lifecycle

Concept
Use Case

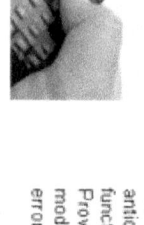

As part of this new product, users will be able to define their TV watching behaviors and be provided with a customized remote that optimally organizes the buttons they will frequently use and eliminate unneeded functions.

Requirements
Risks

Requirement: Users shall be able to use a checklist to define what functions they use (store or on-line).

Requirement: Users shall be able to perform (tasks x,y,z) in 50% less time than using the existing remote.

Risk: Users may not anticipate all the functions they will use. Provide a way to modify in the case of errors.

Design

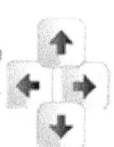

Design a set of remotes with the most probable combinations.

Determine best-arrangement schemes.

Testing

Perform usability testing for preference collection and prototype usage.

Test speed and accuracy of new controls versus current controls.

Training

"This new remote has been de-scoped and optimally arranged according to your usage preferences. All primary buttons are on one remote.

You can add or remove functionality in the future by..."

104

If you are a program or project manager, I challenge you to trade the single person-to-position mindset for that of flexibility across tasks. You will have greater continuity of information across project phases and fewer people idling. As an example, I once was part of a large software development effort where I served as an interface design advisor, a requirements analyst, wrote developer and system interface specifications, participated in system testing, and developed and delivered training to the eventual full-time trainers. This not only reduced the number of people that had to be managed, but added considerable efficiencies and consistency related to re-use of the information common to these efforts. This undoubtedly resulted in cost savings and I gained much personal satisfaction from being productive. Government and businesses should do more flexible thinking along these lines in order to "do more with less".

What about organizations who rely on the strategy of integrating commercial off-the-shelf products; is there any need for taking into account human considerations? The answer again is "yes". In this environment, you may not have immediate and direct control over the interface, but through an up-front analysis and working relationships with vendors you can reach the same result. You also must decide whether the product "fits" your processes, avoiding having to restructure your work around how the software wants you to work. In the situation where multiple products can satisfy functional requirements, usability can be a critical discriminator.

A Detailed Look at Techniques

As was seen in table on systems engineering activities, the field of HSI owns a number of specialized techniques that contribute to the overall systems engineering process. To those unfamiliar with them, they can be intimidating. In order to demystify them, keep in mind that they are similar to other systems engineering techniques in that they are all based on decomposing and analyzing information. Task analysis provides the groundwork for most of the other techniques; it is mainly a decomposition exercise that follows accepted practices. The three techniques discussed below -- user descriptions, usability testing, and use cases -- simply rely on gathering existing and observable information and summarizing it in a manner that is usable by teammates. Of course, although the concept behind these techniques can be easily grasped, the actual execution is better served by practiced professionals. HSI products come in the form of descriptions, risk and requirement statements, design recommendations, performance results, and predictions.

User Descriptions

So, where is the connection between human characteristics and designing a system interface? Why can't we just aim at the general population? Even if we know that there are individual differences among users, what difference would it make in our design? We can only create one interface, so shouldn't it accommodate the majority?

These are all good questions, and sometimes simply designing to the majority is the right thing to do. But for many systems, knowing more about the end users can determine whether a system is usable and successful in the marketplace. As we discussed with the "developer perspective/HSI expert perspective" figure, the idea is to develop a complementary perspective to the technology view to provide new insights about the total human-machine "system". By doing so we may discover ways to make our system usable for more users. Three dimensions that you should consider to accommodate extreme characteristics include expert-novice, young-old, and large-small (height, weight, size of specific body parts such as fingers). In addition, you should examine the environmental conditions that can effect performance. We might determine that our designs need to accommodate the possibility of user clothing (e.g., gloves), endurance, etc.

A technique, creating user descriptions, provides a way to characterize differences between users. This information can then be used to identify situations where human limitations or behaviors may result in performance differences, including errors. Ideally, these should be written in coordination with the concept of operations (CONOPS) and use cases. In this way, user information can be married with situational and environmental factors to create a comprehensive picture of how the system will be used. Having this detail increases the likelihood of better design, communication aids, and safety interventions. Many developers write this activity off, justifying it by saying, "We know who the user is; we don't need to write it down". But a detailed examination of user characteristics can be the key to finding that one "uh-oh" that occurs down the road.

User descriptions can be written in simple narrative and do not need to be highly detailed; details will be brought out later when writing use cases. Rather, the intent is to make the relatively technical and abstract concepts understandable through an action oriented user-centered description. This not only aids developers, but also helps non-developers relate to the system's purpose.

Use Cases and Exceptions – the Key to Designing for Flexibility

Use cases are a powerful analytical technique for interface design. They can provide orientation for people internal and external to the project through rich descriptions of the way people will operate in the system. Detailed goals, human and machine actions, and situational information can be captured for developers. The information can translate into information needed in usability testing, test cases, and training. Use cases should ideally address the comprehensive set of activities people will accomplish with the system, and should emphasize those that are performed most frequently, are most critical, and are most difficult. There is no set standard of what information must be captured in a use case, but some common components include actors, scope, other stakeholders, preconditions to each action, goals, information needs, success scenarios (single statements), and foreseeable exceptions.

An unfortunate mistake that often occurs is that the original concept descriptions address successful "straight and narrow" path use cases, but do not explore exceptions on the basis that the cause of exceptions is somewhat unknowable. Why waste time on something that has an undefined probability of occurring? The failure to anticipate exceptions, combined with all the other stressors in the development process, results in tunnel vision. In addition, use cases must explore the potential exceptions that might occur when using the system. This cannot be understated, as designing for exceptions is the key to making systems acceptable to end users. People want the interface to allow them to proceed in their own way, not to be dictated by an inflexible interface and user manual. To the extent possible, systems should let users perform tasks in various sequences and limit any penalties when they do vary from the norm.

Exceptions are typically a result of two situations. The first occurs when the business logic for "standard" activities does not allow a user to accomplish the task. For example, airlines must anticipate that not all passengers will purchase round trip tickets. They must allow for one way trips, multi-leg trips, multi-leg trips with layovers, etc. The second type of exception occurs when a user performs an action that is unexpected or out of sequence due to personal decision or environmental factors (e.g., unintended user, accident, rain). For example, users should be allowed to lift a gas pump handle and select the gasoline grade before swiping their credit card. A station near my home immediately deactivates the pump, requiring a trip to the line inside the station, if the card swipe is not the first action performed. Granted, there is a sign next to the snack and car wash advertisements indicating that this order should be followed.

The trick is to identify as many of these exceptions as possible before development, and design flexibility into the system. This is often easier said then done, because when it comes to people using machines surprises never cease to exist. This is also a good reason for conducting usability assessments throughout the development lifecycle. You can examine a system thoroughly and include usability experts on the development team. But you will never fail to discover something new when real users become involved.

Recently Askren (2005) published an evolved method for predicting and evaluating foreseeable product misuses. The nine step method involves reviews by subject matter experts and scaling exercises for determining misuse probabilities and risks. This provides a systematic way for manufacturers to greatly reduce the risk to people and property. In addition, in the event of unforeseeable accidents, it provides them with a legal defense showing that they made a legitimate effort to prevent them.

Usability Testing

Usability testing is a technique used to assess what will really happen when human meets system. It is helpful to understand how testing varies, depending on the level of formality and fidelity that are desired or possible. At its highest level of formality, users perform carefully constructed scenarios and their performance is rigorously observed and measured. This may take place in a controlled environment such as a laboratory with one-way glass. This is the classic image most people have. But usability can take many forms, and again, your particular needs and resources will determine what is appropriate. Despite the aura surrounding formal testing performed in laboratories, it can be expensive, logistically difficult, and may not provide the right set of information. This leads many organizations to abandon the practice altogether.

If you would like to conduct testing, don't be dissuaded if a laboratory setting is not practical. It is entirely possible to assess usability in less formal ways. The key point is that some testing is better than nothing. First, costs and scheduling challenges can be reduced by conducting testing in workspaces. As long as you can provide a setting that mimics the product and important surrounding environmental aspects. Most end users will not use products in soundproof booths, so it makes sense to test in more realistic settings. Unless it is critical to record performance measures and user behavior, a lab is probably not necessary. Stopwatches and video cameras provide cheap, but effective substitutes.

Beyond the physical setting, there are a couple of critical things to know when planning usability tests. First, as we saw with training and simulation, a key is to provide an environment containing tasks that are of adequate fidelity and motivating in order to engage the users and promote realistic behavior. This is easier said than done. People use products, and in particular software, for varied reasons and will critically assess scenarios they are asked to perform. If the scenarios or related data do not make sense to them, they will fail to generate internal motivation and instead just play along with the game. This is more so for more specialized and complex tasks such as those requiring high levels of analysis and problem solving. For this reason, creating scenarios and data sets can be one of the most time consuming and difficult aspects of usability test planning.

Second, as discussed in the section on metrics, you must be decisive about what data will be gathered and how you will use them. Especially if you are early in the development process or if you are just attempting to discover user behavior, don't overcomplicate your effort by over-recruiting and measuring performance. In these cases, you are better served by making observations and gathering opinions on a few participants and making quicker changes to the prototype. You hopefully save enough effort to test several times during the lifecycle. In addition, you will be much more appreciated (and less loathed) by the development team. As you get closer to a finished product, determine whether performance measures such as time, errors, and calls for help are useful. If you do decide to measure performance, realize that you need to avoid contaminating the session by encouraging verbal interaction and exploration. I've seen too many efforts that report grossly distorted statistics that are caused by mixing these two objectives. The result usually comes in the form of 1000% improvements from the first to second trial. In this case, the phrase "beware of politicians bearing statistics" can also apply to scientists.

The issue of statistics raises the point that there are several reasons why you might perform a usability test. And your reasons for doing one will dictate the nature of your test. Below are three reasons why you should consider some form of usability testing.

1. <u>Sometimes it is important to measure performance in order to meet requirements or make system comparisons.</u>
   This is true when decisions can cleanly be made based on performance data. Can viewers see quality differences between two televisions? How many seconds should the system allow a user to not respond before cancelling the transaction? Can 99 percent of users complete the task without making a mistake? What type of instructions resulted in better performance? Questions such as these require measurement captured under controlled conditions. This will usually entail more effort, as well as the possibility of introducing artificiality to the tasks of study. For this reason, it is important to avoid taking measurements for the sake of creating numerically based reports.

2. <u>Capabilities, descriptions, and prototypes don't always match user expectations.</u>
   During a product's conceptualization the development team must work against written descriptions, requirements, and their own beliefs of how users will interact with the system. What appears to be on target in the laboratory or factory can be off target when exposed to the real world. Frequently developers discover that their interpretation of a requirement is not congruent with what end users would expect. A good example of how design intentions can fall short can be found in the design of hearing aids. As a user I was encouraged when informed that my first digital aid provided an audio warning when the battery power became low. Previously, I had to keep track of how many days the battery was in use and carry a pack of new batteries. Inevitably I would be caught by surprise and have to deal with no hearing until I could retrieve or buy one. In concept this was great news, except the indicator provided only a five minute warning – way too little time to make an emergency run to a store. I likened this to having an idiot light instead of a fuel gauge, letting a driver know that they have one mile before running out of gas. Usability testing or other investigative techniques may have made the indicator requirements more clear.

3. <u>Conventions and prototypes are helpful, but must be tested for surprises.</u> Again, despite all the effort to conceptualize, analyze, and model, all user interactions simply cannot be anticipated. Usability testing using a diverse set of participants is an efficient way to put the product up to a test. Even experienced usability testers will admit that they never cease to be surprised, even with designs that appear to be sound. As an example, I have noticed that an electronic signature pad in a local store always executed my transaction before I could begin my signature. I made a comment to the clerk who claimed it happens frequently.

One time I realized that due to the position of the pad, I rested my pinkie finger on the edge of the touch surface. That point happened to be close enough to the 'Done' button to trigger it. The signature pad designers followed convention by placing the button in a proper location and by allowing both pen and touch actions, and without testing they would have difficulty anticipating this error.

The ultimate "product" of these techniques is clarity into user characteristics, goals, and experiences. The aim is to develop systems that fit naturally with the way users want them to. Well designed systems provide a tool that works naturally, reducing the attention that the user must expend. Consider two recent contrasting experiences I had using voice recognition systems. Although they both used the same phone technology, my reaction was so different that I had to step back and figure out why. Was it that one could recognize voice commands differently? No, there were no misinterpretations for either. The difference was not the technology itself, but rather the "interface" design. That is, the interface on one allowed me to efficiently attain my goals in a straightforward and efficient process. The other was more of a barrier. Let me elaborate. In the first example, I was paying my Geico car insurance over the phone. The voice menu quickly navigated me to car insurance and after entering my account number, repeated my payment information, and asked if I wanted to draw the payment from the same source as the previous period. Within two minutes I had paid my bill with no stamps, envelopes, or website. The marketing slogan for their website is that it is "so easy a caveman can do it". Well, I would add that their phone payment system is so easy a Ph.D. can do it![3]

---

[3] Ironically, between the time I wrote this example and the time this book went to publication, I have experienced two instances where the voice menu fails to provide feedback on whether the transaction occurred. In one case it did, and in another it didn't. Both required me to contact a person, negating the benefit of automation. This points to the need for continual testing and validation.

Just after that, I needed to speak to someone at a credit card company. After answering several questions and typing in several numbers, I finally reached an operator who proceeded to ask some of the same questions. In this case, my goal was simply to talk to a person. The system (automation and person) not only didn't make achieving that goal faster, it failed to convey the information that I had provided. In essence, the system had zero value and acted as more of a barrier to the customer. And given the fact that they had to ask for the same information, I'm not sure of the reason they wanted the system.

System Engineering Coordination - Legitimizing HSI Through Risks and Requirements

So far we have examined business problems and anecdotal evidence of how knowledge of human abilities and behavior could be of benefit. Some solutions, such as using software design conventions are small-scale and can be implemented immediately. Others, such as establishing performance requirements are solved through empirical study and experimentation. Still others, such as designing controls for weapon systems, are large-scale development projects. For these the information and techniques needed to influence design must be coordinated with other system engineering techniques and disciplines. And to do that, they must be part of the project planning cycle.

Because human systems activities typically exist as a support discipline, it is critical to create a legitimate reason for including it, lest it be considered expendable as soon as budgetary or time constraints occur. Tying itself to the risk and requirements processes is one strategy for strengthening its existence. Why is this important? Because in projects that adhere to systems engineering principles, managers and engineers must account for documented risks and requirements. In the case of risks, the team may choose to develop ways to mitigate or minimize the risk. In the case of requirements, the team must decide how to determine whether the system meets performance criteria. Both processes provide the opportunity for well-defined issues to be floored. While risks and requirements can be unintentionally or intentionally ignored or accepted, they are more likely to be recognized as legitimate aspects of the system development process when put into the context of these processes.

So what exactly are human risks and requirements? In some cases, such as military and transportation systems, safety is an obvious candidate for risk. Here developers should gain a thorough understanding of the physical and mental aspects that contribute to safe operations.

In other cases, such as with software systems, risk may seem to be an irrelevant issue. However, in this and similar settings risk comes in the less subtle form of financial and user behavior risk. This boils down to the fact that if systems are not easy to use, do not support the user in his mission, or are not introduced in the proper way, users will either fail to accept or misuse them. An example of a product that provided functionality, but failed to capture public support is the first cell phone produced by Iridium. During the race to introduce the first cell phones to the general public, they produced a portable phone with wireless satellite service. It failed in the marketplace due to the fact that it was about the size of a brick. When other competitors came out with smaller sleeker phones, Iridium lost out to the public's desire for convenience and appearance. In this case, either the requirements did not constrain its size or they were consciously ignored due to technical issues.

The following two tables outline potential risks on different levels. The first set is on an overall project level and would be of interest to project and program managers as well as marketers and executives. The second set addresses molecular development risks on the level of business rule and design issues.

Project Level Risk Examples	Sample Mitigation Strategies
Users may not accept product or service (P/S)	Include end users and stakeholders in development process – walkthroughs, usability testing. Conduct user forums and iterative usability testing.
Users may not use P/S properly	Conduct usability tests. Follow recognized instructional guidelines. Design so that some exceptional actions cannot be performed.
Users may not trust P/S	Provide performance feedback. Design to allow users to control and cancel actions.
Users may over trust P/S	Clearly state capabilities and limits of product. Design to make system logic accessible.
Users may not use this or similar P/S in the future	Design to make using the system pleasurable. Provide incentives to continue use.
Users may be injured	Conduct usability tests. Follow recognized instructional and warning guidelines. Design so that some exceptional actions cannot be performed.
Users may form a negative perception even if P/S is good	Design to make using the system pleasurable. Allow person to personalize the interface.

Of course, to implement mitigation strategies, we must pinpoint precise instances in the course of product use where risks are likely to occur. This table illustrates this level of risk statement.

Design Level Risk Examples	Sample Mitigation Strategies
Users may ignore product advice concerning next year's tax filing requirements (Turbo Tax).	Provide an explanation of how the product determined that quarterly filings must be performed next year.
Users may perform actions in different sequences (filling station)	Design for flexibility. Program to eliminate action dependencies where practical.
Users may forget to remove their card from the machine (ATM)	Design to reduce risk; card swipe instead of insert and withdraw after transaction.
Users may have difficulty determining the proportion of funds allocated to different accounts (brokerage account statements)	Provide percentages and pie chart by default. Allow user to easily switch to alternative graph visualizations.
Users may have gloves on when using the touch screen	Determine maximum potential button size. Explore various button shapes and tactile feedback to minimize error.

A risk management plan that identifies potential tar pits of user behaviors and acceptance can be equally instrumental for identifying mitigation techniques such as obvious design changes, simulations, end user walkthroughs, and usability testing.

Risk management processes frequently focus on two aspects of risk: the probability of the risk occurring and the impact that an occurrence would have. The thought is that as likelihood and consequence rise, mitigation becomes more important. Mitigation plans are then developed to address particular risks and costs are weighed against the benefits of risk reduction. As an improvement to this, I suggest reporting the ease of mitigation as a third aspect in risk management summaries, if knowable. Often low likelihood and consequence risks will be overlooked due to their lack of importance. But because they can be mitigated easily, they should be dealt with to create a "cleaner" product. This is analogous to misspellings on a software interface. Their consequence is small and therefore is unlikely to raise attention in a list of bug fixes. But by not fixing one or multiple instances of this, which would take little effort, a user's perception is affected by the imperfect product.

Introducing human-related requirements into the requirements management system is another effective way to infuse human systems techniques. Unfortunately, in most requirement documents, human systems requirements are an afterthought -- written by non-HSI persons. For instance, it is common to see the requirement "The system shall conform to XYZ software interface guidelines" or "The system shall conform to MIL STD 1472D". Statements like these are not testable and actually serve to reduce the likelihood of human systems techniques being used. The tricky part about requirements is that they are difficult to define in precise and testable terms. Unless there is a reason for certain human performance criteria to be met (e.g., user must complete a task in a given time period for a specific reason), the requirement will appear contrived and developers will contest their validity. Relating requirements to aspects like satisfaction and acceptance become even vaguer. This is why I advise human systems people to be knowledgeable about the risk management process. It is sometimes easier to express concerns in the form of risks than requirements.

Systems Engineering: Customer Relations

One benefit of usability assessments that goes practically unmentioned is the rapport that gets established between the vendor and customer. This is especially true in the case of custom-made products such as software. I have witnessed firsthand customers accepting software that was delivered late and lacked complete functionality, primarily because they were able to anticipate and appreciate development pitfalls. By participating in usability walkthroughs and assessments, they understood the difficulty of defining and translating their needs into an application. In fact, they realized that they were the source of some issues and took responsibility for shortfalls. Without this rapport, an us-them relationship often develops. The two groups are only aware of their needs and issues, and solvable problems escalate into blameful stand-offs. In the case of off-the-shelf products, where there is no rapport buffer, the vendor and product image suffers when problems arise.

Why Human Systems Integration is Easy

Human systems integration is easy because once it is documented it is fairly understandable to a wide audience. It can be expressed in the form of use cases, narratives or prototypes which can tell a good story. Of course, once you burrow down into the details, there may be some abstraction, but few people on a project need that level of understanding. Sometimes this type of work is really nothing more than going back-to-basics: using analytical techniques to understand the human's role in the system and how to design to accommodate them. Human Factors (the more formal term for what we have been discussing) is often thought of as being nothing more than common sense. And I used to think that for the most part that was true. Now that I've been around the block a few times I know it is more than that. Just as with other professions such as accounting or law, the fundamentals seem straightforward, but there are levels of expertise beyond this baseline that produce better and more efficient approaches, techniques, and solutions.

Why Human Systems Integration is Hard

Being understandable and viewed as common sense has its drawbacks. Because most people have at least some awareness of the approaches involved, this function is often overlooked or delegated to a non-expert or someone else who is "available". As mentioned earlier, this leads to the use of less effective and efficient techniques.

A second important issue is that, like other support disciplines, it is difficult to measure impact and cost-benefits. Since we don't have the luxury of developing parallel systems for the sake of determining the value of design approaches, we are left attempting to make estimates of cost and benefit. The cost in terms of labor isn't too difficult to determine. And sometimes there are measurements such as the required level of customer support translated into dollars or number of product inquiries translated into sales, but how does one place a value on things such as better design, better information for decisions, customer satisfaction and loyalty, quality, etc? These are usually context specific and should be analyzed before the project in an attempt to ascertain the return on investment (ROI).

Another recurrent reason that human systems integration activities do not get included in programs and projects is that they are often absent from the procurement planning process. In the typical government procurement process, a request for proposal outlines the roles, tasks, and level of effort needed to perform the work. The roles and tasks are defined by job titles and one of the criteria proposals are judged by is how compliant the bids are to these specifications. Thus, bidders are hesitant to offer solutions such as human factors or human analyses that fall outside of these descriptions, since it adds to risk of a poor score. In this same manner, they are hesitant to propose solutions that are more efficient via multiple roles since it would not conform to the details in the RFP. Thus, unless capabilities are articulated from the beginning, they are unlikely to be included. The result is that "extraneous" or intangible capabilities such as human factors analysis or usability evaluations are often left out of proposals even though they could add value, even at no cost if flexible thinking was used. This role is then left to the chance of a post hoc sales pitch.

What often gets overlooked in the rush to create work breakdown structures is the fact that people possess skills that can cross-cut multiple job positions. If you are a program or project manager, I challenge you to trade the single person-to-position mindset for a mindset of flexibility across tasks. You will have greater continuity of information across project phases and fewer people idling. As an example, I once was part of a large software development effort where I served as an interface design advisor, a requirements analyst, wrote developer and system interface specifications, participated in system testing, and developed and delivered training to the eventual full-time trainers. This not only reduced the number of people that had to be managed, but added considerable efficiencies and consistency related to re-use of the information common to these efforts. This undoubtedly resulted in cost savings and I gained much personal satisfaction from being productive. Government and businesses should do more flexible thinking along these lines in order to "do more with less".

Systems Engineering Recap

This final chapter provided insight into how to implement the knowledge you have gained about human characteristics in the systems engineering process. We examined several techniques that can be used to understand and convey the way people will use and behave in association with systems, and how this information can be translated into formal requirement and risk statements. You can use these to both plan designs and improve them throughout the development lifecycle. The table showing how human systems integration techniques dovetail into traditional systems engineering activities provides you with a good planning tool.

Key take-aways:
*   Human systems integration (HSI) practitioners can provide insight into user characteristics and behavior that might go unrecognized by developers.
*   HSI techniques can add value to all phases of system development.

- Identifying exceptions to typical system use is critical for improving user acceptance and safety.
- When possible, usability needs should be expressed as risks and requirements in order to fit into the overall engineering plan.

References

Askren, W.G. (2005). Predicting and Evaluating Misuses of Products. Ergonomics in Design, 13(1), 15-24.

Bloom, Benjamin, S., (ed.) (1956). Taxonomy of Educational Objectives: The Classification of Educational Goals: Handbook I, Cognitive Domain. David MacKay Company, Inc. New York.

Collins, J. (2001). Good to Great. HarperCollins Publishers, Inc. New York, NY.

Denison, D.R. & Mishra, A.K. (1995). Toward a Theory of Organizational Culture and Effectiveness. Organizational Science, 6(2) March-April, 204-223.

Fleishman, E. A., & Mumford, M. D. (1991). Evaluating classifications of job behavior: A construct validation of the ability requirement scales. *Personnel Psychology, 44(3)*, 523-575.

Fleishman, E. A., & Reilly, M. E. (1992). *Administrator's guide: FJAS: Fleishman job analysis survey.* Palo Alto, CA: Consulting Psychologists Press.

Gladwell, M. (2005). Blink. Black Bay Books. Boston, MA.

Han, Y.Y., Carcillo, J.A., Venkataraman, S.T., Clark, R.S.B, Watson, R.S, Nguyen, T.C, Bayir, H, Orr, R.A. Unexpected Increased Mortality After Implementation of a Commercially Sold Computerized Physician Order Entry System. (2005). Pediatrics, 116, 1506-1512.

Hancock, P.A., Pepe, A.A., and Murphy, L.L. (2005). Hedonomics: The Power of Positive and Pleasurable Ergonomics. Ergonomics in Design, 13(1), 8-14.

Harvey, R.J. & Hollander, E. Assessing Interrater Agreement in the O*NET. SIOP 2002 papers. In Wilson, M. A. (Chair), *The O*NET: Mend it, or end it?* Symposium presented at the Annual Conference of the Society for Industrial and Organizational Psychology, Toronto.

Helson, H. (1964). Adaptation-level Theory : An Experimental and Systematic Approach to Behavior. Harper & Row. New York.

Merritt, S.M., and Ilgen, D.R. (2008). Not All Trust is Created Equal: Dispositional and History-Based Trust in Human-Automation Interactions. Human Factors, 50(2), 194-210.

Miller, C.A., and Parasuraman, R. (2007). Designing for Flexible Interaction Between Humans and Automation: Delegation Interfaces for Supervisory Control, Human Factors, 49(1), 57-75.

Peterson, N. G., Mumford, M. D., Borman, W. C., Jeanneret, P. R., Fleishman, E. A., & Levin, K. Y. (1997). *O*Net final technical report.* Utah Department of Workforce Services, Contract Number 94-542.

Saucier, G. and Ostendorf, F. (1999). Journal of Personality and Social Psychology, Vol. 76, No. 4, 613-627.

Schmidt, F.L., Hunter, J.E., and Outerbridge, A.N. (1986). The impact of job experience and ability on job knowledge, work sample performance, and supervisory ratings of job performance. Journal of Applied Psychology, 71, 432-439.

Smith, A.F. (2007). The Taboos of Leadership. John Wiley & Sons.

van Gelder, T., Bissett, M., and Cumming, G. Cultivating Expertise in Informal Reasoning. Canadian Journal of Experimental Psychology, 58:2, 142-152.

Washington Post, Metro Seeks Better Ways to Get Word Out to Riders, October 15, 2007, page 1.

<u>Websites</u>:

http://online.onetcenter.org. O*NET-SOC. A website describing a government mandated occupational classification system.

www.baddesigns.com . A website that provides thought-provoking examples of poor interface design.

_www.usability.gov. A website hosted by the U.S. Department of Health and Human Services Office that provides useful interface design guidelines and information about usability testing.

Index

Abilities
   Cognitive 23
   Physical 21
   Psychomotor 22
   Sensory 24
Adaptation 66
Automation 81
   Human Control 82
   Trust 83
   Use and Misuse 84
Behavior 28, 61
Blooms Taxonomy 43
Competence
Instructional
Implementation 48
Customer Satisfaction 72
Examples
   Automated Tax
   Software 84
   Car window Control 97
   Driving Performance 31
   Electronic Signature
   Pad 112
   Finding a Restaurant
   Using the Web 73
   Hearing Aid Battery
   Indicator 112
   Medical Errors 88
   Mental Workload 74
   Real Estate Assessment
   Automation 83
   Roadway Design 59
   Self-service Machines 85

Speed of Technology
   Adaptation 68
   Standard of Living 67
Expertise
   Competency 38
   Instructional
   Implementation 50
   Mastery 39
   Years of Experience 40
General Mental Ability 18
Generational Change 69
Human Behavior
   Design Implications 61
Human Systems
   Integration (HSI) 97
Informal Reasoning 42
Instruction
   Media 44
   Techniques 44
Interests 29
Interface Design
   Exceptions 107
Interface Design
   Guidelines 76
Interface Design Metrics ... 79
Knowledge
   defined 2
KSAO
   definition 2
Machine Interface Design . 73
Measuring KSAOs 32
Organizational Knowledge
   Sharing 53

Other Personal
  Characteristics
    defined............................. 2
Personality......................... 25
  Big Five........................... 26
Personnel Selection............. 9
Requirements 102, 114

Risk Management ... 102, 114
Simulation......................... 52
Skills
  defined............................. 2
Systems Engineering......... 95
Training Implementation .. 47
Usability Testing............. 109

About the Author

Mark Barnes is a contractor residing in northern Virginia. His 25 years of experience includes work in the areas of technology evaluation and insertion, system interface design, training, highway safety research, personnel selection, and statistical analysis.

Dr. Barnes is a member of the Human Factors and Ergonomics Society. He earned a Bachelor's degree in Psychology and Sociology from Central Michigan University and a Doctorate degree in Human Factors Engineering from George Mason University in Fairfax, Virginia.

Parting Notes

I hope you have found this book to be insightful. My intent was to provide useful information for a wide range of applications. If you have comments or questions feel free to contact me at barnesme@verizon.net.

I'd like to thank the numerous professors, co-workers, and organizations that have provided the knowledge and experiences that provide the basis for this book.

I'd like to thank my family for making me realize how wonderful individuals can be and that there is always more to learn.

NOTES

www.ingramcontent.com/pod-product-compliance
Lightning Source LLC
Chambersburg PA
CBHW060628290526
45793CB00001B/185